HAUNTED GARFIELD COUNTY, OKLAHOMA

HAUNTED GARFIELD COUNTY, OKLAHOMA

TAMMY WILSON AND JEFF PROVINE

Haunted America

Published by Haunted America
A Division of The History Press
Charleston, SC
www.historypress.com

First published 2022

Manufactured in the United States

ISBN 9781467151559

Library of Congress Control Number: 2022936639

Tammy:
This is dedicated to all the lovers of history, the adventurers and the storytellers.

Jeff:
For Mom and Dad, thanks for the stories.

CONTENTS

Contents

INTRODUCTION
BORN FROM THE WILD WEST

Documenting the history of the land that would one day be called Garfield County shows that it has been a destination for untold centuries.

Part of the draw of the area was its proximity to the Great Salt Plains, the only place in the world where natural "hourglass" selenite crystals form. Saline groundwater flows just beneath the surface, leftover from the ancient seas that once covered Oklahoma. The evaporating water leaves behind the salt, creating a landscape spread over thousands of acres that looks like freshly fallen snow even in the midst of summer. Animals frequent the area to this day, though none in more numbers than the millions-strong buffalo herds that once ruled the Great Plains. To this day, a few buffalo wallows still rest in the rolling grass of protected pastures around the county.

Native Americans followed the herds and tapped the salt plains for their own needs. When George C. Sibley, head trader at Fort Osage, took his 1811 excursion to inspect hunting grounds, his guides took him on a special detour to visit the salt plains. Inspired, Sibley suggested it become a commercial venture, but the removal of the Cherokee to Indian Territory interrupted development plans. Instead, literal battles broke out over the control of the salt and hunting grounds, which were even touted by Washington Irving in his tour of the prairies when his party of travelers met a group of Cherokee hunters headed that way in 1832. The struggle resulted in a special declaration that the salt plains would be open to use by anyone. Even up to the plains' designation as a national wildlife refuge in 1930, people from as far away as Texas journeyed to gather salt.

While the salt was useful, it made for undrinkable water, which brought travelers farther south to what would be called Government Springs. These natural waters were legendary for not only quenching thirst but carrying mystical healing powers as well. The springs were a well-known destination even before Jesse Chisholm marked out his trail—much of which follows today's Highway 81—for Texas cattlemen to drive their herds up to railheads in Kansas. While most of the cowboys moved on through, paying ten cents a head for the right to cross the Cherokee Outlet, some founded ranching outposts along the way. These would later become stage stations, the first permanent settlements in the open prairie. Many were named after nearby landmarks, and the area gained its eerie first name, "Skeleton Ranch," from Skeleton Creek.

The story of the creek's name is as dark as it is tragic. During the Civil War, the Wichita people journeyed toward Kansas from their reservation in the southwestern part of Indian Territory. The Wichita, having already been pushed out of Texas, were determined to stay with the Union as the war raged around them. Confederate soldiers escorted them across the prairie in 1863, but the escort proved to be disastrous: a strain of cholera broke out from the soldiers. The Wichita died in such numbers that there was no hope of burying them. Survivors moved on, staying in Kansas until returning to their reservation in 1867. For years afterward, human skeletons could be seen lying across the ground at the old camps near the creek, providing a name that would leave a legacy for those lost.

Cattle dominated the next generation of history in the land. As railroads expanded into Texas and ended the need for an eight-hundred-mile cattle drive, more ranchers looked to the wide grasslands for more long-term grazing. It was interchangeably called the "Cherokee Outlet" or the "Cherokee Strip," although the technical Strip was a two-and-a-half-mile surveying error that had mistakenly put the Kansas border too far north. In 1883, several ranchers banded together to incorporate the Cherokee Strip Live Stock Association and leased the whole of the six million acres for an enormous operation. Almost immediately, trouble broke out, as laws had mandated that no improvements could be made to the land, but cowboys set up fences and corrals at various points to protect herds. Arguments about how "permanent" the improvements were meant to be lasted in the courts for years. By then, the cattlemen had another enemy on the plains: boomers.

While much of the attention of the boomers was to "boom" into the Unassigned Lands in the middle of Indian Territory, repeated removal by U.S. Army troops prompted them to turn toward the Cherokee Outlet for settlement. In 1884, David L. Payne attempted a settlement at Rock Falls, and cattlemen were quick to point it out to the army and have him arrested. That settled the boomers for a moment, but growing railroad interest kept the idea of settlement coming. The contract between the Live Stock Association and the Cherokee Nation ended in 1888, and cattlemen hoped for an extension that would keep folks wanting to farm the Strip at bay. Things became even more complicated when a Colorado land syndicate offered to buy the whole Outlet for $3.00 per acre. Ultimately, the federal government stepped in, paid $8.6 million (or a little over $1.40 per acre) for the land, and determined it would be opened by the largest land run in the history of the world.

In September 1893, some 100,000 people congregated along the borders of the territory for their chance at one of the 40,000 parcels of 160-acre farms or smaller town lots in cities that would be founded overnight. The Chicago, Rock Island & Pacific Railroad already ran through the area, completed in 1892 from Wichita, Kansas, down to Fort Worth, Texas. It established depots at "Pondcreek," as it was spelled then; Kremlin (once "Wild Horse" and renamed in honor of the Russian breed of wheat that would come to be the county staple); and on south. Railroad executive M.A. Low didn't care for "Skeleton" on the map, so he replaced it with "Enid," inspired, as the legend goes, from Enid the Fair in Alfred, Lord Tennyson's *The Idylls of the King*. Other legends suggest the name came from various bigwigs' female relatives or an inverted "DINE" sign. Here the story goes that an entrepreneur had started a restaurant out of his wagon and hung up a sign that either fell or was purposely flipped by mischievous cowhands. Either way, it read "ENID."

Enid was to be the prize of the land opening, rivaled only by Alva in the west. This soon-to-be-born town would be the county seat for "O" County, just up the railway from the military base at El Reno and the stage line at Kingfisher and sure to be connected in time to the fast-growing territorial capital, Guthrie. The train scheduled for noon on September 16 planned to leave the Kansas border and with stops at Pondcreek and Kremlin, so the fastest way to get to the new townsite would be on horseback, riding up the old cattle trail from Hennessy.

Even before the time the cannon fired on September 16, the Land Run of 1893 was a debacle. Registration lines at the handful of government offices ran as much as a mile long. Tensions were high among the would-be settlers, and drunken fights broke out frequently. In the east, the starting line became so confused that some runners were three miles ahead of others. Soldiers

Above: The famed before-and-after photographs of Hodge & Prettyman show the anxious energy before and excitement after the noontime cannon. *Courtesy of Wikimedia Foundation.*

Opposite: Many folks who settled what would become Enid rode the Rock Island train, which already ran through the Outlet from Caldwell, Kansas. *Courtesy of Cherokee Strip Regional Heritage Center.*

had to physically hold back protesters, who finally broke ten minutes early. The soldiers opened fire, killing John R. Hill. At the southern line, near Hennessy, settlers mistook the "five-minute warning" shot as the starting gun and burst over the line in such numbers that there was no stopping them.

Once prospectors entered the territory, the dangers were only beginning. The army had set the Outlet on fire days before the run to clear out the brush and any sooners who thought they could hide out, and it was still burning in some places. Runners found themselves facing a line of rabbits, coyotes and snakes making a run of their own fleeing from walls of flames, which soon bore down on the settlers. Even where the burning was done or never started, the land was rough. The only bridges were rail lines, meaning, as Enid native and Pulitzer Prize winner Marquis James recorded his father telling it, "Wagons stuck in the streams and stalled in draws. Rigs broke down from the rough going." Horses gave out or tripped in holes. Passengers bursting from trains at the depots along the way battled human stampedes rushing for townsites.

Enid saw the lion's share of the chaos. The "winner" of the land run was Walter Cook, a scrawny twenty-two-year-old cowboy from the Chickasaw Nation, who edged out from the crowd and staked the 160 acres north of the smaller town lots. As the town was sure to grow, that would be the land that could then be sold piecemeal, likely worth over $1 million in 1911, according to Marquis James. Cook had little time to celebrate, however. Within a few minutes, another runner leaped off his horse to stake the same claim. Then came another. Then another. Then dozens more. The claim-jumpers organized themselves into town lots and called the acreage "Jonesville," working off legal precedent from the 1889 run in Guthrie that had deprived farmers around the swelling town of their larger claims in favor of many smaller claims. Cook later made do, founding a steakhouse and becoming the town's leading bootlegger when Prohibition came with statehood, an activity made easier by his good friends in the courts.

Even after the claims were staked and the weekslong wait for processing at the land office began, Enid had a special breed of troubles that led to war. Since the county seats and railroad depots were all public knowledge before the run, several Cherokee exercised their right to choose allotments from the Outlet and chose them from the valuable land around the Enid depot. Secretary of the Department of the Interior M. Hoke Smith felt he'd been hoodwinked, so he moved the mapped townsite away three miles. After the dust settled from the run, Enid was in two legally distinct areas, Railroad Enid or "North Town" with the depot near where old Skeleton Ranch sat, and Enid or "South Town" as the new county seat.

Lines for registering claims at the land office were so long people often received tickets and were told to come back days later. *Courtesy of Cherokee Strip Regional Heritage Center.*

It made no sense for the train to stop again just three miles after its depot in North Town, so the Rock Island Railroad simply rolled through South Town. Since rails were the lifeblood of the West, people in North Town expected the south to die out and business to drift to the depot. When passengers alighted at the depot and sought transport south, North Town refused them to hasten their rival's demise. If southerners came to pick them up, North Town bandits would cut harnesses and flip wagons. Armed caravans started making regular trips as escorts between the towns.

South Town was awarded the post office, but still the train blew past, tossing mailbags out as it went by. The citizenry of South Town felt they had to fight for their lives. They began hanging red warning lanterns on the tracks to stop the train. Engineers ignored them. They placed dynamite caps and blocks on the tracks. The train revved to plow through them. Then the people of South Town simply started firing guns at the train whenever it came through. The conductors directed passengers to duck below the windows for the duration of the journey through Enid.

It came to a head one July night in 1894 when someone sawed through the supports of the trestle bridge outside Enid. A similar Railroad War had been going in Pond Creek, where citizens had torn up one hundred yards of track and blew up a bridge that spring. Enidites decided to follow suit by rigging the bridge across Boggy Creek to collapse as soon as weight was put

Dozens pose with the wreckage from the Railroad War. *Courtesy of Cherokee Strip Regional Heritage Center.*

on it. The first train through became a spectacular crash with the cars lying at angles in the creek, up the bank and across the right-of-way. It was an unscheduled freight of oil and wheat seed, meaning the passengers on the dawn train were safely stopped instead of being killed. Neither side would back down, so the federal government at last stepped in with a law requiring a depot in each townsite along the railroad.

Though it was born with plenty of commotion, life in Garfield County soon settled down. The first years were rough, and many didn't make it. Farmers struggled with failed experimental crops of tobacco, sorghum, corn and cotton, all made worse by terrible drought, until Hard Red Winter Wheat was found to be the cash crop of the region. Of the estimated 15,000 runners who staked claims in what would become Enid, the town had a population of only 3,500 in the 1900 census seven years later. There had been big dreams of a meatpacking plant that would've been a boon for employment in Enid and farmers across the county, but it didn't pan out and the dream faded. Still, citizens kept their hopes high. An Anti-Knocking Parade was held by Enid boosters in 1911, with a float of a giant symbolic hammer being marched through the streets and buried to encourage people to stop knocking the town with derogatory comments.

High hopes were well met with the discovery of oil. Through the 1910s, Garfield County flourished with an oil boom and high crop prices thanks to the First World War. The county even weathered the Dust Bowl, dodging the worst of the black storms, and made good through the Great Depression with hard work and oil money. In 1938, Enid's position as the rail hub for the entire wheat-producing region set a record by sending out 14,185 train loads of wheat. World War II brought an air base, originally the Air Corps Basic Flying School but today known better as Vance Air Force Base.

Opposite: Though once infamous for the Railroad War, Enid today offers one of the best railroad museums in the nation. *Provine's collection.*

Above: New façades modernized Enid's downtown, showing there is much more to the town than meets the eye. *Provine's collection.*

While fortunes in oil fluctuated to great heights in the '70s and bitter lows in the '50s and '80s, Garfield County always continued its agricultural role feeding the world. Its wheat records continued to climb along with grain elevators being built up on the northeast side of town. The town collected nicknames like "Oklahoma's Queen Wheat City" and "Wheat Capital of the United States." Peaking at a storage capacity of 80 million bushels in 1987, Enid's historic Terminal Grain Elevators district was the largest grain supply in the world for decades and continues to be the largest in the nation.

After being a tourist destination for centuries, Garfield County began with settlement by, as Marquis James called them, "people who for one reason or another had lost out, been run out or weren't doing well enough to suit themselves in places they came from." Diligent folks built up a lasting community that may seem quiet on the outside but bears many secrets in the shadows within.

The first-person accounts in Haunted Garfield County, Oklahoma *are from the experiences of Tammy Wilson.*

1
The Mystery of Bethsheba

While not a ghost story in the traditional sense of a human specter, one spirited legend lingers from the days of the Cherokee Outlet. According to an *Oklahoman* article by Robert Cunningham in 1961, the story of the town of "Bethsheba" (often "Bathsheba") is supposed to have come from a Kansas reporter who was riding through the land after the run, picking up stories of interest. One tale he came across was of particular interest: a town where males were outlawed. Cunningham stated that among the women, "male horses, male chickens, and male hogs were excluded along with the male of their own species." Even having a razor, considered a "masculine implement," was grounds for expulsion from the community. So the legend goes, much of it said to be collected by curious neighboring women who visited the town to learn more, though their husbands "dared not show their faces within shotgun range of the chief of police."

The town was somewhere midway between Perry and Enid, putting it near today's Covington. Though Cunningham quotes the original article extensively, no one these days seems to be able to find an 1893 copy of whatever newspaper it was supposed to have been in. He artfully describes the reporter's second visit as he "rode back toward Bethsheba, wondering if his job was worth dying for," armed with "strong field glasses" to ensure he could spy things out before finding himself too close to a scatter gun.

He came upon a cluster of tents and rough sheds with a group of people, six women all in long black dresses and dark shawls, along with one, the chief of police, who stood in front with a gun trained on him, warning not to come any closer. Despite the distance, the reporter recognized one of the women, later said to be the group's mayor. She was from Kansas, where she had married a "drummer" (or "traveling salesman"), only to find out he was a bigamist with seven kids in another family. Like others in the thirty-three-strong community, she had left the corrupt land of men to start a life in a female-only world.

Cunningham's article relates that the chief of police fired a shot at the reporter but missed, and the women scattered. The brave reporter then sneaked into the town, seeing "a lot of chickens, all hens," "half a dozen mares" and a female dog. The women stayed hidden in tents, watching from afar. The only interview the reporter could get was a farmer who lived by and said that one of his roosters had wandered too close to the town and "the women killed the unlucky fowl with druidistic rites."

The original reporter attempted to end his experience at Bethsheba waxing philosophical about the needs of a crow to a crackle, but Cunningham states that his editor sent him back for more interviews. After riding thirty miles through the countryside from Stillwater, he found the spot empty: no tents, no wagons, no mares. The reporter found someone in a nearby dugout who explained they had all cleared out one night because "they were lonely and afraid." Cunningham concluded, "Bethsheba was gone."

Though the legendary town is certainly not around today, people continue to talk about it. Obviously, the story is problematic, since a town without males would have its agricultural economy ruined within one lost season of baby chicks or calves. Perhaps it was meant to be a joke or a mythological lesson hoping to warn women away from the thought of living without strong, brave men to protect them. John W. Morris in his 1978 *Ghost Towns of Oklahoma* called it "the most peculiar of all ghost towns in Oklahoma." Bethsheba may not have had a post office or been around long enough to be marked in a census, if it existed at all, but it is forever engraved in Oklahoma history.

Perhaps the biggest reason the story continues is, despite the details being all wrong, it is rooted in the truth. A "Bethsheba" of sorts actually did stand in the Cherokee Strip in the Daisy Colony.

Nannita "Kentucky" Daisy (sometimes "Annette" or "Annettta" and "Daisey") came from the late nineteenth-century-era of adventurous female journalists. Like Nellie Bly, Daisy made a name for herself by undertaking daring escapades all for the story. She even outlived her own mistaken obituary in the *New York Times* in 1891 that described her as "a Kentucky girl and a Bohemian in every sense, with a spirit of gentleness in her little body that endeared her to all." While serving as a reporter out of Dallas, she suggested to her editor that she cover the Land Run of 1889. After she arrived in the Unassigned Lands and talked with eager land-seekers, Daisy decided to make the run herself. She reportedly leaped off the train near Edmond before it had even come to a stop at the depot. The story later evolved into Daisy leaping off the train, staking her claim and jumping back on to ride it to the land office. In today's version, as depicted by the Kentucky Daisy statue in Edmond, Daisy was riding the cowcatcher on front of the locomotive with a pistol strapped to her waist when she made her heroic leap.

The real Daisy nearly lived up to her legend. She worked for several years in Guthrie, helping organize public education and offering support to women claiming homesteads. Making another run in 1891 near Chandler, she was shot while successfully holding off claim-jumpers. According to the *New York Times*, Daisy also served as a sooner, setting up an illegal settlement in the Cherokee Outlet in 1892. The article, taken in an interview while she was in El Reno gathering supplies, describes Daisy leading a band of ten women, primarily college educated, creating an encampment in the wooded gulches in the eastern part of the Outlet. Each woman had a rifle, revolver and horse, and they were prepared to evade military troops enforcing sooner laws until such time that the land would be opened to settlement.

Though its standing was not entirely legal, the band apparently did well. Soldiers eventually caught up with them and drove them off, but the ladies returned for the run in '93. They collected a combined capital of $2,500 and—according to the report that was circulated in the *Oklahoman*, *Edmond Sun*, *Cherokee Advocate* and worldwide—successfully claimed three quarter-mile sections for a total of 480 acres west of Ponca City. They built houses and barns, cleared land and took in more settlers, raising their numbers to more than forty. Eventually, however, and like many others, their claim folded. Daisy died in Chicago in 1903.

The truth is that thousands of women made the Land Run of 1893. Many of them were successful, but the would-be town of Daisy didn't make it. According to Aaron Preston, archivist at the Cherokee Strip Regional Heritage Center, not many runners lasted longer than a few years, either selling out once they had their paperwork or going bust in the tough first harvests. Preston said the Oklahoma Historical Society estimates only one in five settlers made it. The Gilded Age dream of a land run proved difficult in reality.

In such an era of experimentation, it's not hard to believe there could have been an experiment like Bethsheba since there actually was one in Daisy.

2

Early Ghost Stories

In *The Cherokee Strip: A Tale of an Oklahoma Boyhood*, Marquis James reminisced about Halloween as a youngster in Enid. Much of his energy was put into the annual Flag Fight, where seniors and sophomores competed against juniors and freshmen to have their flag on top of the high school (then on Broadway) at 4:15 p.m. on Friday after Halloween. It was a game of guile, intrigue and mobs of boys wrestling beneath the trapdoor in the ceiling of the second-floor laboratory to get to the roof. Halloween itself was a less formal affair. James joined "a tough East Side gang which overturned eighteen privies, made off with two buggies and one hayrack, and committed minor depredations. Once we were shot at and to my consternation a member of our gang whipped out a pistol and fired back." It was all in a night's work.

Not everyone leaned toward violence on the holiday. The society page of the 1908 *Enid Daily Eagle* recorded the Halloween weekend's affairs. Amid the fairies, witches and black cats on the streets were a horde of ghosts that popped out from the shadows and around corners. The paper estimated that at least some of them were human and made good to throw shelled corn and gravel at anyone they could find as a target. More unnerving were the ones who stood silent and "insisted on shaking hands with chance passersby," who would then feel the shocking syrupy grip of wet gloves.

Other people kept off the streets at Halloween parties. Hazel Roberts threw a party at 820 West Elm where guests were greeted by a ghost at the door who led them to the fortune-telling room and another ghost who would take them to the jack-o-lantern decorating in the parlor. The Royal Neighbors club had a ghost doorman at its party as well as a ghost parade that rolled through the entire Hayes home. Other parties focused on ghost stories, with each attendant telling a tale. At the Security Club event, there was an extra challenge: each of the ghost stories had to end with the name "Bryan" or "Taft" after the nation's most prominent Democrat and Republican, respectively.

Yet not all ghosts in Enid were content to make their appearances on Halloween. Skeleton Creek, with its ominous name and equally ominous history, soon gathered legends of ghosts appearing at night. Daisy Decker Gregory related that some of the stories were family fiction. While pausing from harvest after a rain, the crew waited on a bridge over Skeleton Creek. Her father started, and the Anderson brothers began telling horrid stories of apparitions to the greenhorns on the work crew. Her uncle came by the house and had all the ladies dress up in bedsheets and sneak up on the crew, letting out terrible wails as they came upon the bridge. Yelling just as loudly, the hired men took off running.

In September 1906, stories circulated that a genuine phantom could be found silently walking the grounds of the north pumping station. Water has long been said to have metaphysical properties, thinning the veil between the material realm and the spirits on the other side. These account for many of the state's dozen or more Crybaby Bridge stories where the cries of an infant lost in a terrible crash can still be heard on quiet nights. Rumors began to spread around town that the new waterworks system had conjured up something that was steadily growing stronger as it came to walk the earth at night.

The first appearances of the phantom were simple glances of a pale figure in the dark. Those who saw it took a second look, only to find nothing. Wondering who could be ambling around the pumping station in the middle of the night, people began to search out the phantom. Some never found anything. Others did find it and fled.

On September 12, the townsfolk were ready to do something about the ghost. The *Wave* reported that "about one hundred and fifty men, women and boys armed with all kinds of weapons from a shot gun to a club assembled in the neighborhood of the 'ghost grounds.'" The weapons were intended to slay the ghost should they find it, but they may also have been security blankets on a dark night, lit only by handheld lanterns and the waning crescent moon. If this all did prove to be a prankster, the weapons would certainly come in handy dealing out justice.

Ultimately, the ghost never showed up. After keeping watch "untill [*sic*] the wee small hours," the crowd stole away. No further references of the ghost could be found, so perhaps it wandered on.

The pumping station ghost was not the only apparition in the early days of Garfield County. After the discovery of oil on the east side of the county just before the First World War, Garber became a boomtown. Its official population tripled from a small depot town on the Enid & Tonkawa Railway to over 1,500 in the 1910s. The unofficial population swelled to untold numbers with roughnecks camping out in fields and makeshift shanty neighborhoods. The promise of fast money brought plenty of ne'er-do-wells to town, and crime was rampant among the transient workers.

A story started spreading that a driller had been murdered for his pay on the road west of town. Even though the tale went through cafés and boardinghouses, the police were flummoxed: no one could find a body. Neither the city police nor the county officials in Enid had any corpse resembling the crime in question. If there were such a crime and no body, how could people have heard about it?

Because the man's ghost was out looking for vengeance.

Along the west road down to the south oil fields, a bloodied figure of a driller roamed. It floated, rather than walked, staring with wild eyes at the people who crossed its path. Those who saw it knew better than to come close. At the end of the road, the driller would take flight and lunge from derrick to derrick. His spirit "reflected light of gas flames, down across the field and back, looking for his murderer." Eventually, the ghost stopped making appearances, perhaps having found the killer or pursued him to a different place.

The *Garber Sentinel* dismissed the story as "some fertile imagination" and suggested a useful ghost would walk down through the red earth to sniff out the oil.

3
COURTHOUSE GHOSTS

Just as the railroad was an invaluable part of a town's success on the Cherokee Strip after the land run, being a county seat gave a community a tremendous head start. Anyone doing legal business would need to register at the courts, making it a destination from the very first, with Enid's hosting of one of the four land offices. Thousands of people came to town, many staying for several days to stand in line to register their claims. Enid's restaurants, saloons and hotels were hopping from the beginning.

The county courts first rented rooms in various buildings, until, in 1896, the first two-story courthouse was built. This proved much too small, so a new Imperial-style courthouse made of Oklahoma granite and Indiana stone opened in 1907. It sat directly in the middle of Broadway, closing the street and allowing Square Park to spread around it. In the early days of Enid, this park was the place to sit in the shade, pitch horseshoes or take a stroll to see who was about town. Life was fairly idyllic until January 29, 1931, when two fires broke out. The Enid fire department worked feverishly alongside Rock Island Railroad employees fighting a fire at the station's grain elevator. Then came another call: the courthouse was on fire. By the time crews were able to contain one fire, the second was a total loss. Fortunately, no lives were lost, as all forty-two prisoners in the jail were freed and given blankets and mattresses to camp out in Square Park for the night.

Federal aid chipped in to build Enid's new, long-lasting courthouse, but arguments with the city nearly made the project miss its deadline. Having the courthouse in the middle of Broadway made for picturesque views down the

Downtown Enid grew quickly, spurred by necessity, with the first county courthouse and jail. *Courtesy of Cherokee Strip Regional Heritage Center.*

street, but automobile traffic demanded a thoroughfare. Finally, an agreement was made to move the courthouse northward, where it is today, opening space for the post office on the south side of Broadway. After years with county government back in rented rooms, the courthouse opened in 1936. Murals by artist Ruth Monro Augur showing historical events in the region such as Coronado's crossing and the land run decorated the halls of the first and second floors. Like the previous one, this new courthouse had its jail on the top floor, where in 1976, brothers Paladine and Burgess Roye added murals with Native Americans, which are now protected by plexiglass.

Tales of historic jails being haunted seem almost as common as theaters or hotels. Even in jails of the new territory's time, ghost stories started quickly. Just a year after the land run, the jail up the rail at Round Pond became haunted by what prisoners and jailors believed was the spirit of a train robber who had been killed when gunfire broke out during his attempted robbery. His clothing had been stored in the top of the cell, a magnet that drew the spirit back. Even after the clothes were removed, prisoners in the cell complained of hearing "a diabolical insane laugh." The jailor, too, heard the laughter, but he could never find anyone inside to make it. Prisoners who tried to sleep in the cell were awakened by being shaken or even strangled by an unseen hand. They finally gave up using the cell for people and kept it as storage.

In 1915, the *Garber Sentinel* reported the county jail in Enid getting its own ghost story. While in his cell with charges of robbing the Garber State Bank, Ed Jackson stopped the jailor during lunch rounds to ask if there might have been a suicide in that cell. The jailor confirmed there had, and Jackson went into a tirade "relating gruesome accounts of seeing ghosts and queer sights there at night." He brought up descriptions of ghostly activity time and again until the jailor made him stop because it was upsetting the other prisoners so much.

To this day, stories of ghosts in the old jail at the top of the county courthouse trickle around. They tell of people hearing coughs or groans from cells with no one inside as well as footsteps and furniture shifting in empty corridors. Shadows appear showing someone walking to and fro, even when the whole floor has been closed for years. Similar poltergeist sounds

Though nearly a century old, Garfield County's courthouse is the most recent of several incarnations. *Provine's collection.*

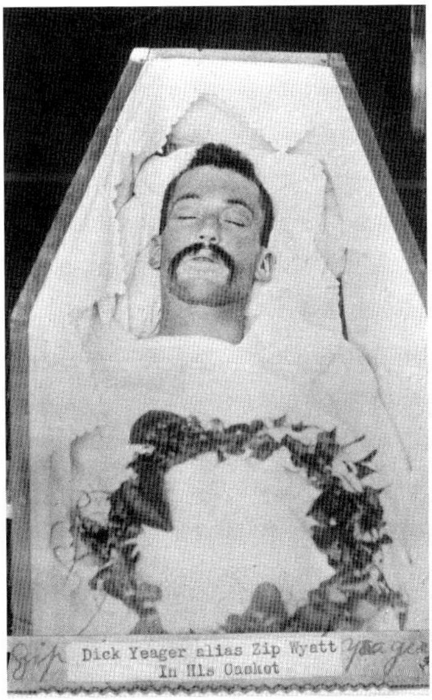

Outlaw Dick Yeager, aka Wild Charlie, aka Nathaniel "Zip" Wyatt is laid to rest. *Courtesy of Cherokee Strip Regional Heritage Center.*

are reported throughout the building, perhaps of one of Garfield County's civil servants still at work despite their body having passed on.

One of the most prominent ghost stories is that the courthouse hosts the ghost of one of Oklahoma Territory's most famous outlaws, Nathaniel Elsworth "Zip" Wyatt, alias Wild Charlie, alias Dick Yeager. He was brought to Enid after 125 days on the run, much of it in the government-reserved Gloss Mountains (or "Gyp Hills" as they were called then) west of town. More than one thousand lawmen and vigilantes in the territory had been after him over those months, including Cheyenne Chief Henry Roman Nose. Once they finally caught him wounded after a shootout hiding in a cornfield, there was some question of what to do with the outlaw. He had killed numerous people in different jurisdictions. Yeager was at least glad to be caught by a sheriff's posse, since he noted, "Thank God for that. Marshals would've killed me." While he lay in jail, different courts vied to try him, and doctors came to marvel that he was still alive with so many bullets inside him, both old and new.

As Yeager waited, the people of Garfield County came to greet him. They rode into town in wagons and on the train, bringing baskets of fried chicken and other gifts. Yeager told wild outlaw stories to anyone that would listen and joked with his lawyers since he'd likely never survive long enough to go to trial. The jailhouse dog liked to lie beside his bed. In Marquis James's memoirs of the Cherokee Strip, he included a tale where he shook hands with Dick Yeager at just four years old. He recalled the tall outlaw was wrapped up in a white sheet with his feet hanging over the end of the cot in a cell that smelled of medicine. When James shook his hand, Yeager told him, "You've shook hands with the biggest outlaw Oklahoma ever had."

After lingering over a month in jail, Yeager passed away after refusing a doctor's suggestion of confession. It makes a great story for his ghost to still dwell in the courthouse jail today, on the run from hell itself, but

Lawmen and keepers pose with Garfield County's first jail. *Courtesy of Cherokee Strip Regional Heritage Center.*

he had never been there. Yeager was caught and died 1895, one year before the courthouse on the square was opened. Likely this was in the old wooden "O County Jail," where the convention center stands today. Then again, who would be able to tell Dick Yeager, alive or not, where his spirit can roam?

4
The First Cemetery in Enid

Driving down Willow Road where Grand Avenue curves along the old run of the Rock Island Railroad brings you to the fenced-in peaceful groves of the Enid Cemetery. If there were any question about what the rows of headstones and markers could be, bold rock signs and the historical iron archway all proclaim "Enid Cemetery" and the year founded, 1897. Folks may not think much of the date other than its pretty lettering, but some do pause as they come to the realization that Enid was founded for the living in 1893. What did folks who passed away do for those four years?

Enid struggled early on to get a cemetery together. Many who died were buried in nearby smaller towns; Carrier was an especially popular final destination once the rail went northeast. Others were buried in family plots on their land, and those with family back East were often taken to be buried in old cemeteries when cooler weather allowed for the transport of a body that far. The *North Enid Tribune* even poked fun at its sister town when an article describing the new cemetery at Round Pond (southern Pond Creek) ended, "Our friends in the south town ought to be as thoughtful."

A potter's field was established on the west side of town at the southwest corner of what is now Van Buren and Owen K. Garriott. This cemetery was on forty acres of school land, meaning it couldn't be sold or used for construction anyway. This solved one problem, though it meant getting approval all the way from Washington. Things eventually were even more complicated since it was technically under Oklahoma Territory jurisdiction and required navigating red tape to do just about anything. Many people were buried without markers, not only to spare the expense but also to avoid getting hung up on legal details. In 1895, the *Weekly Wave* summarized the mayor's address on the state of the city, which implored Enid to take steps toward "procuring land for the benefit of our citizens in burying their dead." The Enid Cemetery Company was chartered in 1897 and started a new cemetery on the east side of town.

Also in 1897, on the north side of town at the Anderson farm, one-year-old Lee Stuart Anderson passed. The Andersons buried him in a little cemetery on their land. Neighbors asked to have their own departed join the Andersons' cemetery, and in early 1898, the family deeded fifteen acres to make an official Enid Cemetery. A few weeks later, the Andersons deeded another ten acres beside it for a Catholic cemetery. A fence once divided the two denominations, but it was removed in the 1920s.

In 1898, the *Weekly Wave* reported decorations for Memorial Day on six graves in "the northwest cemetery, five in the southwest, and one in the southeast." There was trouble with the for-profit cemetery, however, and it soon closed. People were wanting to use the old potter's field for the needs of the living, so it, too, closed. Joe Cummings in the *Enid News & Eagle* cited more than two hundred graves being moved from the original cemetery up to the Enid Cemetery. Other bodies were brought in through the years, allowing families to lie in rest together. The cemetery's marker with the oldest dates belongs to Sam B. Reeves, who passed at the age of four in 1865.

Though bodies were moved, there is the ongoing understanding that not everyone was disinterred. Even among those with markers, some were dug up and found to be only an arm and a leg. Troubles kept going on after the official end of the old potter's field, such as in 1897 when W.H. Crawford, who had leased the quarter section where the old cemetery lay, took a piece of fence that had been left behind to make a corn crib. The fence had once surrounded the grave of Marshal Williams, whose body had been shipped to Boston, and then it was moved to Kate Gregg's brother's grave. Crawford had thought it was abandoned, but Gregg promised her brother was still using it. No one knows who else has never left the old potter's field.

That first cemetery's most famous resident was likely the outlaw Dick Yeager, and reports say that he's still there. After dying from his wounds in the county jail, Yeager was taken to the potter's field in a quiet procession. He was buried without a marker, both from some folks feeling a murderous outlaw didn't deserve such a thing in a potter's field and because a famous outlaw's grave would be a goldmine to souvenir-seekers. Since there was no

Today Champlain Park and a quiet neighborhood, this patch was once Enid's first cemetery. *Provine's collection.*

marker when the move to the new cemetery began, no one found him, and no one gave him a marker in the north, either.

Today the land that had once been a potter's field is the Kisner Heights addition, featuring the acclaimed Midgley Museum that houses the collections of world travelers and big-game hunters Dan and Libby Midgley. It is popularly known as the "Rock House" thanks to its custom façade assembled by stonemasons from the rocks collected by the Midgleys through the years. Many of them were Oklahoma-found, including the three-and-a-half-ton petrified tree from Woodward and selenite-encrusted fireplace from the Salt Plains.

Neighbors in Kisner Heights report all things quiet on what was once a graveyard. Stories tell of construction workers digging up whole caskets when laying foundations, but those were all disinterred peacefully. Jarrett Crosley at the Midgley Museum—itself sometimes whispered to be haunted with the residual energy of the Midgleys' expeditions—said he's never heard of any spooky tales about it. Instead, the urban legend of a ghost from the old potter's field leans toward Champlain Park. There's said to be a man in

The "Rock House," also known as the Midgley Museum, is one of Enid's hallmarks. *Provine's collection.*

a cowboy hat who hangs out there, strolling and sitting by himself. Seeing a cowboy hat is nothing out of the ordinary in Enid, but the man's clothes, too, are decades out of date and dirty as if he'd just ridden in from the range. Stranger still is that he disappears as soon as those who see him approach.

Cummings suggested in his look back at Dick Yeager's last days that this cowboy might be the outlaw himself, including a spectral horse. He wrote, "If on a moonlit night, you find yourself in Kisner Heights and hear the clomping of horse hoofs and the soft sounds of a harmonica floating in the air, don't be afraid. It is just ol' Zip Wyatt roaming free off into the light."

5

THE CURIOUS CASE OF DAVID E. GEORGE

The mystery started small in 1903, as shown in a short obituary in the newspapers, such as the January 14 *Enid Echo* stating among the recently deceased that "David E. George died very suddenly at the Grave Avenue hotel yesterday. He is supposed to be a man of considerable property, and recently made a will. A coroners inquest is being held by Judge Jacobs."

The statement was simple enough, although those who knew George had questions. What was a man of considerable property doing having drifted into town, officially a house painter (an occupation travelers often proclaimed to avoid vagrancy laws), but always trying to get people to buy him drinks by singing, doing comedy routines or reciting Shakespeare? William H. Ryan, who served as Enid's mayor from 1921 to 1923, knew him. He'd also known it wasn't Shakespeare, but Tennyson, as the stranger crooned out, "Come not when I am dead, to shed thy tears around my head." Ryan admitted in an interview that they "did not know much about Shakespeare in those days," but the words were pretty enough to treat the man to a drink to soothe his throat after.

By January 15, the *Enid Weekly Wave* seemingly had laid the matter to rest. While the legal process was still finalizing details, George's death was "no doubt a suicide." George had purchased strychnine from Watrous-Harley's drugstore, saying it was to "kill a d——d hound," and then purchased more strychnine later when that clerk had left. George E. Smith, a friend from Iowa, telegraphed that he would arrive soon to claim the body. That

The body of David E. George is posed lifelike to show the quality embalming. *Courtesy of Cherokee Strip Regional Heritage Center.*

A room is set aside showing what would have been David E. George's last moments of life. *Provine's collection.*

could have been the end of it all, but within a week, the story had become front-page news with the possibility that George was none other than John Wilkes Booth, Lincoln's assassin, on the run under various aliases for nearly four decades.

Before Smith arrived, Ida Harper of El Reno did. She had been an acquaintance of George when he lived in a home with Mr. and Mrs. J.W. Simmons in a house he had bought for $350 and invited them to stay in exchange for cooking and cleaning. While Harper visited Mrs. Simmons one afternoon, George came home, greeted the ladies in the front room and then went to his bedroom. Soon he called out to them, saying he was very sick and seeking company for his passing. George said he didn't want a doctor, but Simmons called for one anyway and made him strong coffee for some vitality. While he sipped it, George said he needed to make a confession. As the *Echo* quoted Simmons quoting George, "I am the man who killed President Lincoln, he was a good man—Mrs. Suratt was entirely innocent as was the man killed in the barn and one other. I caused the death of four people, have not seen a moments peace since." He told of escaping to Europe by hiding in a trunk on a ship and then traveling in "secluded places" for many years before returning to the States.

George then fell unconscious, and they thought he had died, likely from morphine overdose. Then George awoke, recovered and later asked Mrs. Harper if he had mentioned any strange stories while in his stupor. Mrs. Harper, nervous about how he might react, "assured him that he had not." George seemed satisfied, but he left town soon after, giving the Simmonses the house in exchange for a simple promissory note.

Upon his arrival from Iowa, Smith spun a tale of his eighteen months of friendship with George, enough to be his executor and beneficiary of a $2,500 life insurance policy. He told of George's scholarly work on Shakespeare and his extensive travels to the Holy Land, Assyria, Europe and Africa. Smith said that he had never heard anything of George being John Wilkes Booth. When the will was opened, it was found to be "not worth the paper it is written on." It was, in fact, one of many wills filled with outlandish property claims and fictional family members. Smith left Enid and the body behind.

Though the *Weekly Wave* proclaimed it did not believe "that it is probable that David E. George...was the remains of J. Wilkes Booth," it provided ample "indisputable circumstantial evidence." Citing the December 1901 issue of *Medicinal Monthly Journal* that gave a report of numerous "murderers of presidents of the United States and European potentates," the editor and reporters quoted, "The head and forehead of J. Wilkes Booth was kephalonord. The ears excessively and abnormally developed; inclined to the so called satanic type. The eyes were small, sunken and unequally placed. The nose was normal. The facial bones and jaw were arrested in development and there was a partial V-shape dental arch." Enid's Dr. McElrath examined the corpse at Penniman's Funeral Parlor and found all the marks the same. Hundreds of other Enidites went to Penniman's to consider the remains for themselves, to the point that Penniman had to announce the body was going to be locked up in cold storage.

People began to compare notes. George had always carried himself like someone well-to-do, even though he was obviously poor. He limped, too, on a leg that had been broken at some point, just like the story of Booth's escape and treatment by Dr. Samuel Mudd. Booth was born in 1839 and shot Lincoln at only twenty-six years old. If Booth had lived to arrive in Enid in 1902, he would be about sixty-three years old, which is what several people claimed George had mentioned in conversation about his age. The

Atlanta Constitution once cited Booth living in Mississippi; hadn't George had mentioned living in Mississippi about six years? Back in 1898, J.W. Booth's brother Dr. Joseph Booth had responded to a newspaper that said the assassin was spotted in Brazil with, "South America! Why, the last we heard of him he was in Oklahoma." W.F. Green, a painter from Hennessey, who had worked with George on a varnishing job after George had fallen, said George mentioned that he was Booth. Green had taken the story as "hot air" until others said the same and so likewise reported his tale to the *Garfield County Democrat*.

As word spread through newspapers across the country, more stories of Booth started coming out. There were plenty of legends already about what had happened to Booth after the assassination of Lincoln. On the official record, Booth broke his leg leaping from the theater box where he had shot the president but still managed to slip out the back and ride on a getaway horse as he had planned. Along with David Herold, Booth grabbed their stock of weapons at Surratt's Tavern and rode through rural Maryland, stopping to have his leg set by Dr. Mudd. For days, he was living in the woods before crossing the Potomac to Virginia. Military pursuers tracked Booth and Herold to the farm of Richard H. Garrett. Herold surrendered, but Booth stayed hidden in the tobacco barn. Soldiers set fire to the barn to draw him out, and Sergeant Thomas "Boston" Corbett shot Booth despite standing orders for his live capture. The body was given an autopsy at the Washington Navy Yard and then buried in an unmarked grave among the Booth family at Green Mount Cemetery, Baltimore, Maryland.

Yet there were those who questioned the record. Several soldiers at the Garrett farm said the body pulled from the barn had red hair and a freckled completion, not at all like Booth's dark hair and ready-for-stage clear skin. Discrepancies in the autopsy report were said to be from Booth's ten days on the run. Senator Charles Sumner argued against paying out reward money, not because it was part of a military action, but rather that they hadn't got the right man. Newspapers appealed to the federal government for a statement, but the government replied with a simple summary of the official events from 1865.

For the most part, people grew tired of the story. C.M. Clark told newspapers that David E. George had visited him in Oklahoma City some time before, staying as he was a friend of Clark's brother from their time together on General Bedford Forrest's staff during the Civil War. In fact, Clark claimed Forrest was George's brother-in-law, though few people believed that, either. Marquis James's editor was done with the story, even though James had cooked up a great article feeding information to mediums who had come to Enid to parlay with the spirit of whoever it was in Penniman's Funeral Parlor.

Penniman had entertained thousands of curious visitors, reportedly for five cents each, by propping up the embalmed body with its eyes open and looking comfortable in an armchair. With no one to claim the body, courts were looking to place it into Penniman's care along with the deceased's final possessions inside his old trunk. Penniman took this as a great opportunity to showcase his embalming techniques with long-lasting arsenic concoctions.

Soon after, Finis L. Bates, a Tennessean practicing law in Texas, arrived in Enid to add another chapter to the strange tale. Bates, as he later wrote in his book *The Escape and Suicide of John Wilkes Booth*, met one John St. Helen in 1872 in Granbury (spelled "Grandberry" in his book). He was just starting out his practice, defending a man for selling tobacco and whiskey without a license. The client wanted John St. Helen as a witness in his defense, but St. Helen was hesitant to come to court. St. Helen seemed nervous, wheezing as he asked legal questions, yet his vocabulary and pronunciation were those of a trained dramatist rather than someone living in a log cabin in frontier Texas. Once St. Helen was absolutely certain that a retainer fee swore Bates to secrecy as his lawyer, St. Helen paid him and said, "My true name is not John St. Helen."

The mystery intrigued Bates, who struck up a friendship with the stranger. St. Helen was a Shakespeare enthusiast and loved to quote Tennyson, even giving acting advice to young traveling performers. Bates took elocution classes from him to improve his public speaking. When St. Helen fell deathly ill in June 1877, Bates visited him to offer some comfort to the emaciated and weak man. St. Helen believed he was nearing the end of his days, so he confessed, "My name is John Wilkes Booth, and I am the assassin of President Lincoln. Get the picture of myself from under my pillow. I leave it with you for my future identification. Notify my brother Edwin Booth of New York City."

St. Helen fainted away, and Bates took the tintype photograph as requested. St. Helen recovered, however, and soon met Bates as nervous as he had been years before when they had first met. He asked, "Do you remember anything I said to you when I was sick?" Bates replied he did. St. Helen reminded Bates that it had to be kept secret as his lawyer. Bates, far more amused than convinced of the whole thing, agreed that it was a secret and offered St. Helen the chance to tell his whole story. St. Helen, relieved, did.

It was a wild tale of the assassination conspiracy actually being organized by Vice President Johnson to protect Southerners from a vengeful Reconstruction. Following the slaying, Booth had taken specific roads guarded by soldiers who allowed him through with a password. The man killed at Garrett's farm was a farm overseer named Ruddy who was carrying Booth's papers; Booth had fled into the woods. Without those papers, Booth had thousands of dollars in gold stashed in Canadian banks that he couldn't get to. Instead, Booth slipped through West Virginia and Kentucky claiming to be a wounded Confederate soldier trying to get home. He'd wandered through the West ever since, going as far as San Francisco before looping back to Texas.

The man said guilt haunted him for the co-conspirators who had been executed. Bates couldn't accept the story and even suggested that St. Helen turn himself in since there was no real way to prove it. St. Helen refused, so Bates simply replied, "I must continue to know you as John St. Helen." The two remained acquaintances and later drifted apart when St. Helen moved on to Leadville, Colorado, in 1878. Bates moved back to Tennessee to pursue law there, but the strange story always stayed with him.

It came to mind again when he saw an 1897 testimony in the *Boston Globe* by former general David Dana, who always suspected Booth had gotten away. Following his hunch after the war, Dana met a man named Treadkell in Nebraska who said he'd traveled to Utah with a well-spoken teamster who didn't know a thing about harnessing mules. Treadkell later bought a book about Lincoln's assassination and saw the photograph of John Wilkes Booth, which he said was the spitting image of the "Jesse Smith" he'd known. Bates wrote to Dana, and the two carried on a correspondence that persuaded Bates that there may have been some truth to John St. Helen's tale.

Bates came to Enid to see the body of David E. George and proclaimed he was very much the man he knew in Texas, merely some fifteen years older and, of course, embalmed. He gave two days of speeches in the Enid opera house about the whole thing, with admission at twenty-five, thirty-five or fifty cents depending on the show. Bates even reached out to Treadkell, who happened to have moved to Garfield County, to come into Enid and see the body. Treadkell arrived and agreed that the body and the tintype that Bates always carried with him since collecting it from St. Helen both looked like Jesse Smith.

Putting his legal skills to work, Bates got in touch with the Booth family, who claimed custody of the corpse (now a mummy). Bates bought it from them and took George on the road, giving lectures and leasing the mummy to carnivals. He even offered $1,000 to anyone who could prove the body was not that of John Wilkes Booth. No one received the award.

After Bates died in 1923, his widow sold the mummy. It traveled across the country, coming up in the news periodically with updates touting its authenticity. Doctors analyzed it in 1931 in Chicago, taking X-rays and saying that the leg break and scars matched the known description of John Wilkes Booth. Researcher David Farris noted in *More Mysterious Oklahoma* that the mummy had been sighted in Ohio and Pennsylvania in the 1960s, but soon after the trail had gone cold. George's mummy may have been destroyed, or it may be sitting quietly in some collector's attic, waiting to be found again.

Versions of the mummy story have grown to say that it wasn't only Booth's body that remained in Enid but also his ghost. The building that was once Grand Avenue Hotel has been restructured along with much of the block into today's Garfield Furniture. Proprietor Russ Frazee welcomes visitors to see the room upstairs where George passed and offers free postcards featuring the famed photograph of George's mummy.

Though it has housed many businesses in its long life, the Frazee building now hosts Garfield Furniture. *Provine's collection.*

Strange noises haunt what was once the hotel, now storage for the furniture store. Echoing footsteps from unseen feet are creepy enough, but stranger are the sounds of doors slamming in a space where all of the doors were removed years before. Most terrifying of all is the sharp cry and painful wail of a man's voice as in the last moments of life. Both upstairs and down among the furniture, people get the feeling of someone standing behind them. Some have even gone as far as to say they've felt cold hands pressing down on their shoulders and the backs of their necks. Motion sensor cameras are often tripped in the middle of the night when the building is empty of any living soul.

The paranormal investigation show *Ghost Lab* performed experiments there in 2009, hoping to capture some real evidence. A few EVPs and some sensations were all they could gather, hinting some force may be there. Nothing proved that it could be Booth, George carrying on a tall tale in the afterlife or some other former tenant of the Grand Avenue Hotel that may still be taking up residence.

Even if it were Booth, he would have to be splitting his time with the Granbury Opera House in Texas, where they keep a seat empty during every performance for the ghost of John St. Helen. This of course feeds into Booth's love of the theater, although the opera house wasn't built until a few years after St. Helen left Hood County.

As odd as it is to have Booth in Enid, it is even odder that there is a *second* legend with yet another player from Garrett's Farm in town.

While newspapers were debating the story of George and Booth, a new question arose: Why Enid of all places? The reporters at the *Wave* supposed that it was from older newspaper reports about Enid's struggle to find a permanent city cemetery in the early days, since George told the hotel landlord "that if he was found dead just to throw him out the back way." Perhaps he wanted a place where his body might not be found. Or perhaps it was simply the next town for George to meander up the railway. Or it may have been an effort to get closer to the conspiracy—rumors were that Boston Corbett had come to town, too.

Following the shooting at the Garrett farm, Corbett was court-martialed for shooting against order. Corbett maintained he felt Booth planned to blast his way out and acted in self-defense. Secretary of War Edwin Stanton agreed and laid the matter to rest. Corbett then tried to move on, although he was haunted by death threats in the mail and offers of gifts, including one of Booth's pistols. He took up a position as a doorkeeper at the state legislature of Kansas but, after pulling his gun in response to a disparaging comment, went to stay at the Topeka Asylum for the Insane. On May 26, 1888, Corbett stole a horse and escaped. He may have disappeared to Mexico or died in the Great Hinckley Fire in Minnesota in 1894, but some say he became a patent medicine salesman working for a time in Enid, Oklahoma Territory. He may have even been buried in an unmarked grave in Enid Cemetery. Booth could well have been trying to find the one man who could commiserate about their experience in one of the most tragic moments of American history.

Of course, the *Weekly Wave* gave only sixteen-to-one odds that David E. George was actually John Wilkes Booth.

6
Ghost Signs at Alton Mercantile

Samuel Alton was an astute businessman who had grocery wholesaler companies in both Iowa and Kansas. When he learned the territories south of Kansas were opening up, he wanted in on the action. Even before statehood, Enid was a bustling city in O Territory, so Alton decided to put a grocery wholesale business right in the center of it. Built in 1902, Alton Mercantile was described as "the most modern structure of its kind in the southwest" and cost about $40,000. Samuel Alton was the president, and his son, Harry, was the secretary and manager. Harry became a leading businessman in town as the approachable "city dude out of a magazine" with features "handsome, decisive, and cold." He carried off Frances "Blossom" Fleming, daughter of banker Oliver J. Fleming, in what Marquis James called "the most widely advertised courtship in the history of Enid." The romance came to a tragic end with Blossom's youthful death in 1911.

Alton Mercantile traded in a great many products. It housed the Alton Candy Company, which went through eight train cars of shelled peanuts a year, as well as the Alton Broom Company, which produced nearly 200,000 brooms a year—Oklahoma being the largest broom corn grower in the country. Besides candy and brooms, the mercantile also had cocoa, pancake flour, extracts, tea, spices, flour, canned fruits and vegetables, canned oysters, chocolate, raisins, olive oil, pickles, macaroni, gelatin, vinegar, rice, soda, powdered sugar, cornstarch, tapioca, syrup, soap and more. Alton Mercantile roasted its own brand of coffee, manufactured peanut butter and

Alton Mercantile stands as a bastion of Enid commerce from the early days. *Courtesy of Cherokee Strip Regional Heritage Center.*

was a distributor for companies that made tires, tobacco, chewing gum, shoe polish and cigars.

An interesting aside about the candy-making days comes from K.P. Simpson, who later opened his own mercantile in downtown Enid. The children's groups in town would regularly tour the candy company, and one day young Simpson attended a tour. As he watched the candy being made, he witnessed a huge bucket of something red that looked alive being poured into the trough. Upon closer inspection, he realized it was thousands of red bugs that were being smashed by a roller and strained to color the candy red—cochineal bugs from Mexico!

Alton Mercantile was quite successful, but on the night of February 12, 1924, Harry called a meeting at his house located at 1212 West Broadway with H.H. Champlin, the president of First National Bank, and H.G. McKeever, a local attorney, to discuss the finances of the mercantile. Mr. Alton's new wife and son were out of town, and the men met around 11:00 p.m. Within minutes of leaving, both men were notified that Harry had shot himself in the head. McKeever made a statement that they were planning to meet the next day to figure out a plan of action for the financial issues, and he thought they had covered everything satisfactorily. Upon examination of the books, however, it turned out that Mr. Alton's assets far outweighed his liabilities. His friends thought perhaps his bad health had undermined his mind. The real reason for the suicide has never been discovered.

The Alton Mercantile company was taken over by Alton's partner H.A. Marr, and later the building became a Sears Warehouse. It was purchased by Leonardo's Children's Museum in December 1992.

Over the years, it became rumored that the complex of Alton buildings was haunted. The urban legend was that Harry Alton hanged himself in one of the buildings, but the true story is that he shot himself in his home on West Broadway. That is not to say that Alton may not still be wandering the halls of his beloved mercantile. There have been many reports of eerie occurrences, and though the stories come from several different people, they have striking similarities.

One former Leonardo's employee was there late one night, having gone in alone and set the alarm so they knew there was no one else in the building. Yet they reported they could hear footsteps upstairs, and the internal phones started ringing. They claim they were never scared but wholeheartedly believe the building is host to the spirit they felt many times. They described it as not necessarily scary, more sad or lonely, and that it would only happen when they were there alone.

Another former employee often worked alone late at night. One night she heard the distinct sound of footsteps coming from the third floor above her. Scared, she called her husband to come stay with her. When they were leaving for the night, they set the alarm and the motion detector went off on the third floor. They went up to investigate and discovered the back door was open. They could not have set the alarm if it were open. What could have set off the motion detector if nothing was there?

On another occasion, one of the art instructors who worked there came in on a Monday when the museum was closed to the public. She was painting a mural in the back of the gift shop when she heard the front door click. She turned around to see who was coming in: a figure in white with straight dark hair, just shy of hitting the shoulders. She assumed it was her boss at the time, so she didn't think much of it. About an hour later, she went upstairs and noticed the side door was locked. This confirmed that the person she had seen earlier must have indeed been her boss, because no one else was tall with dark hair and the door was locked, so it could not have been someone off the street. She went to her boss's office and was satisfied to find her there. But her boss was in a black turtleneck dress, and her hair was pulled back—not at all like what she'd seen earlier. She asked if she had changed clothes. She stated she had not. She asked her boss if anyone else were there. She stated they were the only two in the building as far as she knew. The instructor continued pressing her boss, asking her if she was sure she didn't see someone else come in an hour earlier. Her boss assured her she had not, and they were the only ones there. She told her boss about seeing someone dressed in white walk through the museum. The two then scouted the museum together and found they were, indeed, alone.

The same instructor reported she would get frustrated when she would walk into her office to retrieve a book or file she needed for a class, knowing it would be on her desk where she had left it, only to find it would be gone. She would yell out, "Alton! I need that book! I have a class in thirty minutes." She would then walk away and come back a few minutes later, and the once missing book or folder would be back on her desk right by her keyboard.

After several instances of strange occurrences, the instructor began comparing stories with the janitor of the building. They both worked by themselves either hours before anyone came in or hours after the museum closed. They found they had both experienced hearing footsteps on the third floor when they knew for certain they were alone in the building. She said, "It was clear as day—footsteps from one end of the building to the other—not just a creak here and there."

The instructor went on to tell the story about her dog also experiencing the ghost at Leonardo's. She had to make a trip to the museum around 10:00 p.m. to turn the kilns up like she had done numerous times before. This night, she decided to take her black lab along for the ride. They entered the side door. Her dog ignored the animal room and stayed by her side. They approached the open space by the elevator, and the dog stopped dead in his tracks. He looked to the left, and the hair on his back stood on end. She tried calling him out of his trance, but his gaze remained fixed and he lowered his head. His behavior scared her, and she pulled him to the pottery lab with her. On the way back through the museum to leave, the dog once again hesitated by the elevator and would only walk past if he was up against the wall, head down, tail tucked and she was on his right side. As soon as they got away from that area, he was completely back to normal.

Several claims of witnessing a ghost include seeing a man in white on the third floor. Yet another former worker confirmed this and said, "Yes, I saw him. We used to keep the costumes for Dynamos on the third floor, and one day I was up there by myself getting costumes, and I turned around and saw a man in white, like a butcher's or grocer's outfit, standing there. When I looked again, he was gone."

Ghost signs still show on the cleaned façade of the Alton Building. *Wilson's collection.*

The Gaslight Theatre troupe originally took up residence in what is now the annex at Leonardo's. There are stories of odd things happening to them, too. A local artist tells a story about when she was invited to do an art show there. Upon arrival, she checked out her surroundings and found the theater was dark and empty. She began hanging up her pictures, but as she was working, she heard a thunderous boom from the theater. She went to see what it was, but there was nothing there. She hurriedly finished setting up and left.

One night, there was going to be a concert, and the sound technicians had worked hard to get everything just right, but when it came time for sound check, there was no sound. They set about troubleshooting and realized a piece of equipment had come unplugged. They plugged it back in and tried

Above: Further ghost signs show the Alton building's many careers through the decades. *Provine's collection.*

Right: The back of the Alton building is a spooky enough place to begin a ghost tour. *Wilson's collection.*

again. Still nothing. They did another check, and this time another piece of equipment that had been plugged in just minutes before was unplugged. This happened several times, each time it being a different piece of equipment. The thing was—they were the only ones in the building.

Ghostly evidence is even visible from the outside of the Alton building. The front of the building has been painted over many times, yet the "Alton" keeps showing through no matter how many times it gets painted over. "Ghost signs" such as these are common on historical buildings, such as the warehouses of Bricktown in Oklahoma City, where later businesses might power-wash off the old resident's name painted on the brick. The scientific explanation is that the old paint bleeds to appear again, but it is something else entirely for "Alton" to push its way through a repainted façade.

There is another building that was once part of the Alton complex that is now an industrial supply company. People there have witnessed the transparent figure of a man in the halls and have reported smelling cigar smoke. They have named him Harry.

In the 120 years since the Alton building was erected, it's been many different things, but one thing remains the same—the ghost of Harry Alton still shows up for work.

7
Murder Three Times
The Corner of Grand and Broadway

The source of this story is a history of the Enid Police Department that was put together for the department by the wife of a longtime member of the police force, Stephanie Galusha. This is my version of that story in my own words, but I wanted to credit the woman who originally published the history.

The city of Enid is over one hundred years old—older than the state itself—and in all that time, only three police officers have died in the line of duty. The odd part of this statistic is that all three deaths happened on the same corner of downtown outside of today's Paramount Realty building.

E.C. Williams came to Enid when the Cherokee Strip was opened, and he became the city marshal. Enid was bustling as it grew, generally cordial, though a few feuds broke out. J.L. Isenberg was the owner of the *Enid Daily Wave*, a decidedly Democratic newspaper. R.W. Patterson, registrar of the U.S. Land Office, was also known to be a Democrat; however, the business of the land office went to a different newspaper called the *Tribune-Democrat*. This angered Isenberg a great deal, and he set out to sully Patterson's reputation by printing unflattering stories about him in the *Wave*. As time progressed, the articles became more and more inflammatory, and Patterson's anger became unbearable.

On June 26, 1895, Patterson sought out Isenberg to settle the score once and for all. The two men met at the corner of Grand and Broadway and commenced to scuffle. Gunshots rang out—Patterson had shot at Isenberg but missed. Isenberg ran to the safety of a nearby store, and Patterson continued to chase him.

Marshal Williams arrived on the scene. He was no great friend to Isenberg, who had dubbed the marshal "Tammany Williams," suggesting the corruption of the Tweed Ring, and editorialized the marshal's hastiness to shoot in his papers. Nonetheless, Williams was a lawman, so he tried to stop Patterson. In his fury, Patterson turned his gun on Williams and wounded him horribly. Williams charged ahead in his attempt to bring Patterson to his senses. He shot at Patterson, hitting him in the temple and killing him instantly, proving, as Marquis James wrote, that Enid had never seen a better snap shot. Williams died of his wounds shortly thereafter.

Isenberg was never harmed, though two men died because of his actions. He ended up eventually leaving Enid and moving to California.

Nearly eleven years later, Marshal Thomas Radford became the second enforcer of local law to be slain in the course of his duties. Being a strict lawman, he'd managed to alienate a citizen named John Cannon. Now Cannon was not a stranger to law enforcement, but not in the way one would think. He had once been the county jailor. There was a particular woman of ill repute who spent an inordinate amount of time in jail because of her occupation. He fell in love, married and opened a rooming house with her. Not surprisingly, the rooming house garnered the reputation of being a brothel, and the police looked in on them quite a bit.

Cannon had been heard making threats about killing Marshal Radford, but Radford's next plan set the deed in motion. Radford, unhappy with Cannon's "business," had it shut down and forced the tenants out. Cannon then attempted to reopen across the street by renting the rooms at the Coney Island Saloon. Radford caught wind of this and forbade the owner to rent to Cannon. Cannon was furious and set out to get even.

Marshal Radford was at the Tony Faust Saloon inside the Anheuser Busch Building, warming himself at the radiator and talking with his friend George Mulkin about the cold weather. Cannon entered the bar through the back door, walked up to Radford, and said, "Bad day, isn't it?" Then he stuck a .38-caliber revolver to Radford's chest and shot him. Radford ran, but he was shot two more times, in the back and then the head, before he finally collapsed on the sidewalk outside. He did not die immediately, instead some thirty minutes later, but he never regained consciousness after the last bullet hit him in the head.

Cannon called the county sheriff to confess what he'd done. He was arrested and placed in the Grant County jail in Pond Creek due to the fact that the citizens of Enid were outraged by the death of one of the best lawmen they'd had to date. In fact, Radford was officially the best, as the chairman of the police committee proclaimed him as such in a 1905 city council meeting. Enid citizens would likely be moved to violence if they had access to Cannon.

Things became more peaceful in Enid until a hot July night in 1936, when a local tavern owner and former police officer, Jim O'Neal, got word that his bar may be robbed. He was being extra watchful of all who entered his establishment.

A man came in and took a seat at one of the booths to have a beer. Two women were waiting outside, and he motioned for them to come in. After some time, O'Neal felt confident that he had seen this man in some pictures, so he summoned the authorities.

Officers Cal Palmer and Ralph Knarr arrived and approached the man, asking him to come with them. The man asked to finish his beer. They obliged. After he chugged the last gulps, he sat the empty stein on the table and produced a gun he'd hidden next to him. When he opened fire, Palmer was killed instantly. An innocent bystander and Knarr were both hit as well; Knarr survived and later became chief of police.

The shooter fled the bar and ran down an alley, where he jumped into a car occupied by Fred Caldwell and Dr. L.D. Huff. He directed them to drive. Caldwell proceeded forward, and when he saw police officers coming at them with their guns drawn, he and Huff opened their doors and bailed out, leaving only the shooter in the car.

Officers converged on the man; he fled the car and hid behind it for a shootout. A fatal shot to the head finally took him down. The man was traced to a local hotel where he had been staying with another man for some time. Police captured the second man, Donald Reeder, and learned that the shooter's name was Lawrence DeVol and that he had been the trigger man for the Karpis-Barker Gang. Sixteen people had escaped from the St. Peter, Minnesota Hospital for the Criminally Insane, and Reeder, DeVol and one other man had been the last of them. Reeder was returned to Kansas, where he was wanted for bank robbery and being a habitual criminal.

It's not all that unusual for police officers to be killed in the line of duty, and luckily Enid has only lost three. The curious twist to their stories is that they died on the *same* street corner, the corner of Grand and Broadway, several years apart. The corner has since become a bit of a superstition among the Enid Police Department, and it might be wise for bystanders, too, to take a little extra care traveling there.

8
Around Downtown

From the beginning, Enid's downtown has been lively. It earned the nickname the "White Way" from the electric streetlights that illuminated boardwalks and streets where the after-supper crowd would promenade for some air, either on foot, in buggies, riding Enid's one-time streetcar or even in automobiles, like the Oldsmobile owned by Herschel Goltry, the first automobile in town. Much of that boisterous energy still continues, even from some folks who have passed on.

105 North Grand

Paramount Realty has had some odd goings-on in its historic building. Before it hosted Paramount, it was home to Surety Abstract, but most of us remember it as Lambert's, a high-end dress shop. Before it was Lambert's, it was a department store called Herzberg's.

Dennette Ray, owner of Surety Abstract, jokingly made a comment to a longtime Enid attorney that they thought the building might be haunted. They had witnessed several strange occurrences like glimpses of people who weren't there and hearing furniture moving even though nothing was out of place. While they watched, unseen hands knocked stacks of things off the counter and file cabinets would open that were closed only minutes earlier. An employee and her young child were alone in the building one Saturday.

A postcard view of Enid's downtown in the 1930s. *Courtesy Metropolitan Library System.*

The woman heard her child talking to someone, and she went to find them, as there was not supposed to be anyone else there. She asked who they were talking to, and the child said, "That man right over there." There was no man. They were unable to explain these things any other way. The attorney thought for a moment and stated he didn't really know why it would be haunted. They finished their business, and he returned to his office only to return a short time later with an old newspaper article and declared, "You know, it just might be haunted."

A 1956 newspaper article relayed the story of a woman who worked in the Herzberg Department Store. Her estranged ex-husband came into the store one afternoon as she worked, demanding she give him seventy dollars for a dentist visit. She refused, and he gunned her down and turned the gun on himself, right there in the store. Ray had not been aware of this story until she saw the article.

The Eerie Oklahoma paranormal investigation team was allowed to inspect the historic downtown building, and they were not disappointed. There was a light at the back exit that seemed to flicker and act strangely all night. The team asked the owners if that were normal. We were assured it was not. Later, while we were sitting on the floor in the area of the shooting, one of the members reacted to something moving behind her and touching her. I had also looked up because I thought I saw something, but, alas, there was nothing there.

As the investigative team wandered around on the main floor of the big building, we heard noise coming from upstairs. It sounded as if someone were moving something heavy, like furniture or something. I was going toward the stairs to see if it was the other part of the group, but they came walking up the stairs from the basement. None of us had been upstairs at all!

Always wanting to know as much as I can about a location, I interviewed the children of Dick Lambertz, previous owner of the building. His daughter, Brooke Reed, and her brother, Matt Lambertz, stated that, as children, they found every possible nook and cranny of the old building to play hide and seek in and never had any ghostly encounters. They did say they got spooked by the mannequins more than once.

Another brother, Gant Lambertz, is of the opinion it could be the jolly spirit of Dick Lambertz, who is by far the most interesting character to have ever possessed the building:

> *This is the large building to the south that Lambert's occupied in its last years of existence where Dick held an auction one week prior to his passing to "get all his affairs in order." This was not the building with the mannequins. The air conditioner and the elevator always had a squeak, which could explain the noises heard from the first floor. The "haunting" that could be going on could be all the older ladies hitting on the handsome Dick Lambertz in the better place that they all now share.*

The current inhabitants at Paramount Realty contend they still have frequent occurrences and claim it is indeed, very, very haunted.

SIMPSON'S MERCANTILE

Simpson's Mercantile is just around the corner on East Randolph. K.P. Simpson originally sold military surplus out of the back of a Jeep before he was able to get into a building to open his store, Simpson's War Surplus, in 1946. After a little while, he was able to purchase the current Simpson's building. It is a huge three-story structure where everyone in Enid bought jeans and work shoes for decades. K.P. had two sons, Rick and Larry, who became part of the family business, all three running the store together.

In the 1980s, they began airing commercials on local television. In each commercial, someone would ask a question about whether they would ever be able to get this or that product from Simpson's, and the answer was always, "'T ain't likely!" The punchline became locally famous, and Enid folks still use it to this day. The Simpsons expanded their writing, directing and acting into several western movies that star Enid people in family-friendly Old West stories. They even used part of the building to build sets for the movies.

K.P. Simpson passed away in 2000, but some say he continued to show up to work at Simpson's Mercantile. The store sprawled over several hundred square feet, and the offices were on the second-floor loft that overlooked the store. After K.P.'s passing, employees reported seeing him standing up there, watching over the store just as he had done so many times before.

Another report came from a longtime friend of the family and character actor in their Western movies. He was at the store one day, visiting with the two brothers. The doors to the store were open, and the three of them were standing there visiting when he felt someone tap him on the back of the shoulder. He turned to see who it was, and the brothers asked what he

Window paintings and hoof prints on the sidewalk welcome guests to Simpson's. *Provine's collection.*

was doing. He told them someone had tapped him on the shoulder. They laughed and assured him there was no one behind him.

After some time, the brothers phased out the store and created Simpson's Old Time Museum. Over the years, they had collected an enormous amount of Western memorabilia, so it seemed a natural progression. One interesting item they have in the museum is a newspaper article chronicling Dollie Douthitt's infamous courtroom shootout along with the pistol she used to do it.

Larry Simpson passed in late 2021, and Rick is now the sole curator of the Simpson's legacy in Enid.

Blood Brothers Tattoo

Just a block from the square at 123 East Broadway is another family endeavor: Blood Brothers Tattoo, owned by Chris and Tanner Bodelle. The first known business to occupy the building was the City Bakery in 1910, with Mrs. Lesta Lason's Furnished Rooms occupying the upstairs. It later became various furniture companies and other small businesses, but it is believed that regardless of whatever businesses were downstairs, the upstairs was a brothel.

The brothers began noticing that when only one of them was in the shop, weird things would happen. Chris stores his ink on a shelf with a lip that makes it impossible to fall out, yet he would find ink bottles lying several feet away on the floor. Tanner's ink bottles are on a small cart, and there is a good foot of space between the bottle and the edge of the cart, yet he would have the same thing happen. Neither said anything for a while, and one day they were standing at the back of the shop near Tanner's desk talking about it when a water bottle flew off the desk and landed between them.

One night, Chris locked the front door, turned off the lights and was making the long walk across the shotgun building to the back door to go home when he saw a woman on the mezzanine. She was wearing a black dress with lace. Chris explained in detail the lace and the embroidered edges. He was quite shaken and left quickly. Sometime later, he was having a discussion with the previous tenant, and she asked him if he'd seen the lady on the second floor yet.

Chris was on the phone with an insurance agent one morning when he was alone in the shop, and as he was talking, he was shushed by someone he could not see.

Art at Blood Brothers brings new life into one of Enid's oldest buildings. *Provine's collection.*

Objects going missing is one thing, but reappearing is something else. One day, Tanner placed his keys on his desk, and they went missing. He looked all over for them and eventually came across them lying in the middle of the floor where he had walked several times during his search.

The Bodelles do not have access to the third floor, which is secured with a locked glass door. Even though it's supposed to be empty, sometimes noises trickle down like someone moving up there. One day they found the door wide open, and the owner of the building, the only one with keys, questioned if they had been up there. They had not; they couldn't have been.

Something spooky happens there about every week or two, so whoever is still hanging out at 123 East Broadway is quite persistent.

9
DOLLIE DOUTHITT

J.T. and Dollie Douthitt were prominent landowners in early Garfield County. They staked a claim on the south edge of Enid and built a home where the Enid Police Station is located today. The boundaries of their property were what are now Van Buren, Frantz, Washington and Owen K. Garriott Streets. Enid High School now sits where their grand farm, replete with orchards, once stood.

On April 24, 1904, Dollie Douthitt shot her husband during a quarrel. He lived long enough after she shot him to refuse to testify against her, telling authorities it was his fault that she shot him in the first place. He claimed his actions had made her jealous.

Not much is known about the facts surrounding the shooting. One account says she found him romancing a hired girl in the barn, and another states they argued when he came home late and she was just suspicious. Either way, she shot him, and he died. He left her their property with one contingency: she never remarry.

The Douthitt Chronicle by Dennis Porter recounts what has become the most famous Dollie Douthitt tale, but due to the risqué nature of the story and that it involved a prominent businessman, it appears that it did not make newspaper headlines. The story goes that Dollie became involved with a married man, and they would rendezvous in the rooms above his downtown business. One evening after their regular tryst, he told her they could not go on meeting. This angered her a great deal, so, when he fell asleep, she sharpened a straight razor and "slashed him in the area of her discontent."

He awoke screaming and ran from the building. He came across a paperboy making his early morning rounds and finally landed at the University Hospital, where he was nursed through the night. He lived through the ordeal, though their relationship ended.

Dollie had garnered the reputation of being a loose cannon, but her next round of shenanigans sealed it for eternity. She had to appear in court for an unpaid roof debt. She represented herself because, even though she personally found her court-appointed attorneys to be kind men, she was suspicious that they would not have her best interests at heart. During the hearing, it is said she screamed, "You fiends! You sons of bitches! I will get you all!" before she pulled a pistol from her waist and shot up the courtroom. She shot U.S. commissioner Harry Wedgwood, the attorney for the Ready Roofing Company, nearly killing him, but he lived to be the principal witness against her at her trial. She also shot at Judge Sutton from Alva; the bullet grazed his coat arm. She then shot at a young attorney in the courtroom, Roy Elam, who threw files in her face, which distracted her long enough for him to escape her wrath.

Douthitt was later determined to be insane and not accountable for her actions. She was exiled from Enid after receiving treatment in a mental institution. The joke in the legal community became that Dollie set the limits for permissive behavior in Enid: you could kill your husband and castrate your lover, but if you shoot a lawyer, you must leave forever.

Individual markers show members of the Douthitt family buried together. *Wilson's collection.*

Dollie was said to have wanted the most beautiful headstone in all of Enid. *Wilson's collection.*

In 1935, Dollie was released from the hospital and lived out the rest of her days in California. She was reinstated to competency by the court in 1938 and died at the age of eighty-two. Her body was returned to Enid, where she was buried in the family plot.

It was said that Dollie had stated she would have the biggest tombstone in the cemetery, and indeed she does. She rests under the tallest monument in the Enid Cemetery—an angel with eyes that seem to watch anyone that comes near.

Dollie was not the only colorful Douthitt. Her daughter, Mona Loma Thelma Pearl Douthitt Hourihan, visited several pharmacies trying to secure cyanide. Once she did, she returned home, killed her husband and took the cyanide. She left a lengthy suicide note, and because it contained the disposition of debts and property, it was considered her Last Will and Testament and therefore appears in all the abstracts of the houses in the Douthitt Addition in Enid. Her suicide note reads as follows:

Dearest Tookie:

Please don't be sad, or grieve when you get this—just be glad for me—'cause I'll be out of my misery—no more pain or disappointments—and you know, Tookie, I'd have to die sometime and now is so much better than later. Life & man are such disappointments—and Jack cares naught for me or he would not lie to me & chase woman. I really feel at times as tho I were losing my mind and the thots of being like Dorthy (and my health together) is more than I can stand—so that's the reason I'm taking the easy short route out.

I'm sorry for all the trouble I've been to you but surely do appreciate all you've done for me—which has been awful lots. Wish I could have repaid a part of your goodness to me. You've always been my best friend as well as sister and mother to me.

I got the cyanide this AM. Had the deuce of a time too—went to 6 drug stores, before I could get it.

I sadly regret all the money I wasted in the past 3 years. He wasn't worth a lick of it, either. Took—I want you to have everything that's left. There's a balance of $153. Due on the car. 3 payments of $45.00. One of the payments past due. Gen. Motors Accept. Corp. Detroit, Mich. The receipts for the car are in the brown grip. The life ins. Policies were never paid up but don't suppose you could collect on them if they were.

I don't want any extra expense on the funeral—just the cheapest possible—please—my blue dress is what I want to be put away in (and my wedding ring and blue bears)—and Jack has plenty of clothes. His gray suit looks nice on him—Please see that he wears that, will you please? And bury us together. Give Leedee the balance of his clothes—that Jake can't use. Oh yes, Jacks chest & about $30 or $40 of tools are at the Baker Hemphill job. Ask Supt. Snodgrass or the lather Dick Rogers for them.

My wardrobe trunk (nothing due on it) is at Mrs. Ora Lindsay—704 N. St. Paul St., Dallas, Texas. (The keys to both trunks are in the little cedar chest. Almost everything is in the car.) Give Mrs. Lindsay my last regards. (She called us "her kids".) We owe $4.20 to Mrs. Kruse 701 N. Ervay St., Dallas for 12 meals. Our rent is paid in advance. Well, this is *all I can think of now. Oh yes, mama has a policy on me that will cover all expenses, doesn't she? Don't cry—just be glad I'm happy & out of all pain and disappointments.*

Goodbye—Love—your ornery little sis.

Loma

(Jakeita—I want you to have the piano & tolls and the diamond when you're 18)

Jakeita—Dearest Little Sweetheart:

Forgive me for not sending your red shoes & dress for your birthday—but Dearie, I just didn't have the money. Tell Tookie to make over these dresses for you—(the ones she & your grandmother can't wear). Well, Dear Heart, be a good girl & don't cry for your auntie—scause she will be happy—not sick any more.

Love,

Your Aunt Loma

Mon. 1:10 PM

Jack has $24.00 due him and $10.25 RR fare and owes Dick Rogers $15.00 borrowed money—that's all—I wanted to wait until the end of the week but this misery is more than I can endure.

Goodbye—Loma

While there are not any specific ghost stories about the Douthitt ladies, they certainly live on in Enid's folklore.

10

Broadway Tower of Terror

Enid's Broadway Tower has been the downtown skyline's trademark fourteen-story art deco office building since its completion in 1931. The tower was made in the height of style with its cast-iron ornaments and terra-cotta geometric zigzags and sunrises. It has been home to numerous businesses over the years and was even used as the temporary county courthouse in the 1930s after the second burned. It was purchased in 2012 with intentions of turning it into a hotel, at which time most of the businesses moved to other premises. The hotel work was never completed, and the building now stands empty, looming over the 100 block of East Broadway.

The Broadway Tower has two elevators, one of which was one of the last manually operated elevators in town. One woman ran the elevator in the morning, and a second one ran it in the afternoon. The afternoon operator also stayed after hours to clean several of the offices, including the law library located on the twelfth floor. This was an L-shaped room where the doors opened into the short leg of the L where sat two oak reading tables, furnished with brass banker lamps with green glass shades. Bookshelves full of law books went to the ceiling. Around the corner, the long leg of the L was home to a long conference table where client meetings and depositions would be held. Because of the confidential nature of law offices, and since the doors could not be seen from that area, sleigh bells

The Broadway Tower stood as Enid's tallest building for nearly a century. *Provine's collection.*

had been hung on the door so the parties could hear whenever someone came into the library and cease private conversations.

One evening, the elevator operator was cleaning the law library, vacuuming the area where the conference table was. She backed around the corner to the reading tables and was startled by an elderly gentleman reading a law book by the light of one of the lamps at one of the tables. She turned off the vacuum and began apologizing profusely for disturbing his reading. She hadn't been aware anyone had come in. She turned to collect her things, and when she turned back around, there was no man, no book and no light on. She hurriedly pulled the vacuum out by the cord, bouncing it off the bookshelves as it went.

When the building was occupied, there were several law offices there. I was a paralegal for the one on the eleventh floor. After learning the story about the man in the law library, I questioned the bookkeeper about whether she had experienced anything strange, as her office was a tiny room in the corner of the library. She said she would often hear the sleigh bells jingle as they did when someone came in, but there would not be anyone there.

One afternoon I received a call from another paralegal in the law office on the third floor. I assumed it was to discuss a case, but she asked, "What do you know about this building?" I asked what she meant. She asked, "Is it haunted?" At the time, I knew the story about the man in the library and I said as much. She asked if I had ever heard anything about the third floor. I had not. She said, "Well, they probably won't admit it if you ask them, but two of the attorneys just saw a man walk through the wall of the office."

On questioning one of the attorneys who had been in the building for over forty years about why the building might possibly be haunted, it was discovered that there was an account of someone dying in the elevator shaft.

According to an article in the *Enid Events* newspaper, about 5:00 a.m. on Tuesday, February 1, 1933, the body of A.L. Thorlton, the night engineer for the Broadway Tower, was discovered by cleaning women. The doctors examining the body concluded the tragedy had happened around 3:00 a.m. Thorlton was apparently in the habit of leaving the elevator door propped open so he could easily pop in whenever he received the signal to carry women working in the building from one floor to another. He had just received such a signal when he switched off the light and stepped into the open shaft. The elevator cage had slipped up to the fourteenth floor in his absence. No one worried at first, but about two hours later, the women called the night watchman, and the search was made.

Is the man reading in the law library one of the old residents of the building? Does A.L. Thorlton still wander from floor to floor? It certainly appears there is a good reason for the building to be haunted.

11
Schoolhouse Haunts

When people start whispering of ghostly tales around town, the Enid High School Auditorium frequently comes up. Legends say that it was built atop an ancient Native burial ground, though no archaeological evidence ever appeared during the construction in 1953. Staff who have served as far back as 1971 say they've never heard or seen anything. Former students, however, talk about hearing the creak of seats folding and unfolding during practices even without an audience. Others claimed to hear footsteps sounding on empty aisles. Even without anyone nearby the switches, lights would shut off, and those left off would be turned on. Ghost stories in theaters are so popular across the state (and nation and world) that it may be that spirits like to take in a show. The tradition of the "ghost light" keeps the spirits at bay when productions are on to prevent anything unseen tampering with sets left onstage overnight, though skeptics point to it as superstition.

For an unquestioned spooky school story, Longfellow Middle School offers Enid's best. The legend goes that in the late 1920s or early '30s, not long after the building was opened in 1923, a student was working in the science laboratory room on the east side of the second floor. Something went wrong, and an explosion broke out. The student may not have lived to complete the experiment, but his spirit goes on playing at the school.

Numerous expansions have added space to Longfellow, including a fallout shelter from the days of the Cold War. Though there are stories of the ghost boy straying to explore the newer parts of the building, most have him

Something spooky is said to roam the halls of Longfellow. *Provine's collection.*

hanging around the oldest part of the school. Most common are the sounds of footsteps running through the seemingly empty hall. Several people at the school after hours have heard the sounds and been puzzled at a child still being there so late. More puzzling is that the footsteps aren't the squeak of typical sneakers but the slap of old-style leather soles against the flooring. When they go out to check the hallway, they find it completely empty.

An even more unsettling sound is the recurrent "boom" from the old science lab. The first time people hear it, they hurry to see what emergency has happened and instead find all things quiet. It seems the sound is a residual occurrence replaying the event that made the ghost wander the Longfellow halls.

Beyond sounds, stories tell of physical action performed by the mischievous ghost boy. Books sometimes fall off shelves, which is a reasonable occurrence if the shelf is uneven, and of course people working in a school may find books on shelves rearranged. It is stranger to watch a single book shift as if on its own, sometimes falling and sometimes moving to a new position between other books. Lockers are known to open and close all by themselves, as if someone unseen were peeking inside. One former staff member heard the sound of slamming metal and went to check, finding the locker doors moving one by one down the row. As soon as they cried out, though, the doors stopped. Other staff members have watched room doors open, even ones they were certain that they had locked. They heard the rattle of the handle and watched the door open, expecting to see someone walk inside. Instead, the door stands alone.

There are those who have even claimed to catch a glimpse of the phantom boy. They say they never see him long, either sitting in a classroom or walking down the hall. At first, they take him to be a regular student, even though it is far past time for students to be in the building and he is wearing trousers and a button-up shirt that might be considered dress clothes in today's style. If they try to get a better look or even blink, he's gone but surely not forgotten.

It's fitting to have a ghost in the school named for Longfellow, whose lithograph portrait hangs in the foyer. His poem "Haunted Houses" from 1858 reads

There are more guests at table than the hosts
Invited; the illuminated hall
Is thronged with quiet, inoffensive ghosts,
As silent as the pictures on the wall.

That makes for a good reminder of the souls who came before us, many of whom might still be walking among us.

12

The Follower at Waukomis Cemetery

When it becomes time to whisper about ghost stories in Waukomis, most people point toward the old school. Built in 1933, it was then the *new* school, built directly on top of the old one from 1915 that was demolished to use as a foundation. As classes transitioned to today's facilities, this one was left behind along with all the residual energy of generations of students. Those who gain permission to explore the mothballed hallowed halls say they can still hear numerous footsteps in empty classrooms, lockers slamming shut and basketballs bouncing on the gymnasium floor.

Others point to the Waukomis Cemetery for their local urban legend, specifically what they like to call "the Follower." The legend goes that those who walk through the cemetery get the sensation of someone walking after them, following first from a distance and then moving closer. When the visitor turns to look back, there is no one else among the neat rows of headstones. They decide it must have been the Oklahoma wind stirring the grass, making it sound like there were footsteps after them. Upon going on, the footsteps come back, following closer and closer until they sound like they're coming from a person right behind them. They even have the feeling of someone being right there with them. If they haven't moved on already, they may feel something else, like a cold hand on their arm or shoulder. There may even be the tickle of someone's breath on the backs of their necks. Usually that is enough to have folks move on.

There does not seem to be an answer for who, or what, the Follower might be. The cemetery is the final resting place of hundreds of people, including

People walking amid the rows of headstones in Waukomis Cemetery get the feeling of being followed. *Provine's collection.*

several notable former residents of Garfield County. Congressman John N. "Happy" Camp, who represented Oklahoma's Sixth District from 1969 to 1975, lies near the marker for Medal of Honor recipient Lieutenant Colonel L.R. Vance, for whom Vance Air Force Base was named. Vance earned his medal aboard a B-24 bomber that sustained heavy damage, piloting it alone after ordering the rest of the crew to bail out. Vance survived, ditching the plane in the English Channel to ensure that everyone, including the injured radio operator, could escape. Flying back to the United States afterward, his C-54 transport disappeared over the North Atlantic.

Perhaps one of the residents of the cemetery has decided to get up for a stroll alongside visitors rather than rest, albeit in an unseen spiritual form. While there may be several suggestions on who the Follower is, there is one person it surely couldn't be—Lewis W. Wilkins. The reason is simple: he was too tall for anyone to feel his breath on the backs of their neck. Wilkins rightfully earned the title "Oklahoma Giant" by growing to be eight feet, two inches tall (some newspapers reported as much as "8 feet, 9 inches in his stocking feet").

Lewis Wilkins, Jr. - Waukomis Giant - Picture from Wardie Wilkins, nephew. His father took Claim southwest of Waukomis in Run. Born 1869 - Died 1902. 8 ft. 2 inches tall (6 ft. man standing under his arm), Weight 365 lbs., Waist 58", Shoe size #24, Glove size #16, Hat size #8½. Tallest known man in the World at time of his death.

Lewis Wilkins stood eight feet, two inches, well earning the title of "Oklahoma Giant."
Courtesy of Cherokee Strip Regional Heritage Center.

Wilkins was born in 1869, one of six children, and quickly outpaced his siblings in height, as he achieved six feet tall before age twelve. He was healthy and active, especially enjoying wrestling since there was no one who could come close to his weight class. The family moved to a farm outside Waukomis in 1893, and by then Wilkins was already traveling to perform in circuses and fairs as officially the tallest man in the world. Enid newspapers kept locals abreast of his journeys all across Europe, reporting postcards from Switzerland and Paris. In 1902, however, Wilkins returned home suffering eyesight problems. Doctors discovered a brain tumor pushing on the back of his eyes, the same tumor that had caused his overabundance of growth hormone. When Wilkins tragically passed away a few months later, there was an offer of $25,000 (some $800,000 in today's money) for his body, but the family turned it down. Lewis Wilkins had been responsible with his showbiz earnings, leaving behind more than $40,000 of worldly value to his family. After a viewing and funeral of more than two thousand people as well as a procession through Waukomis, Wilkins was laid to rest in the cemetery.

An interesting sidenote of the tallest man in Oklahoma being buried in Grant County is that the smallest man in Oklahoma is buried just nine miles directly west in the Del Norte Cemetery outside Drummond. Baron Nicu de Barcsy was born in 1885 in Budapest, the son of an aristocrat cavalry officer. He was less than two pounds at birth and grew to an adult height of thirty-five inches. After his birth, his mother the baroness experienced a hormonal shift that caused her to grow a rich brown beard. Not deterred, the senior baron, himself nearly four hundred pounds with very little fat, brought them into the circus with himself as the manager and strong man, his bearded wife and their small son. "Little Nick," as he became known to English-speaking audiences, would perform atop his father's open palm. After his father's death, Little Nick and his mother toured with the Campbell Brothers circus, which wintered near Drummond. The de Barcsies liked it enough to settle there, and Little Nick was a prominent member of the community, giving performances as fundraisers with the Elks Lodge, until his passing in 1976.

13
At the Knox

Grand, mysterious buildings seem to swell with untold stories, and there are few buildings grander or hinting at more mystery than the elegant tower at the corner of Washington and Broadway. It's gone by many names through its century standing watch on its corner. Older folks still remember it as the Masonic Temple. Today many usually call it the Knox Building after longtime owner Charles Knox, though quite a few like to refer to it as "Enid Symphony Hall." Whatever someone calls the building, whenever the name is said, there's almost a whisper to the words, as the temperature seems to drop a degree.

The Masons have been a part of Enid from the very beginning, with a formal lodge being pronounced in 1894 just a few months after the run. Territorial Lodge No. 19 grew to become today's No. 80, a far step from its humble early days getting meeting space from the International Order of the Odd Fellows in exchange for janitorial work. By the turn of the century, the Masons had their own temple at 126 Independence. Fortunes continued to grow, and soon the members of both Enid Lodge No. 80 and Garfield Lodge No. 501 hoped for a bigger temple. In 1921, they began to sell bonds hoping to raise funds for a three- or even four-story building. With oil money flowing in Roaring Twenties Oklahoma, they funded their five-story new temple.

Irony swooped in: all that oil money also meant that everyone else was looking to build, such as the convention hall and the American National Bank building. Contractors had to subcontract, and building supplies could be found only by clever buyers willing to look where others didn't. Despite the slowdown, the new temple was completed that summer, boasting ready

Enid's Symphony Hall still bears the marks of the Masons. *Provine's collection.*

tenants of the Johnson-Brown Furniture Company and Henninger Royer Undertaking Parlors on the lower floors.

Glory days eventually fade, and Enid's golden glow of wealth began to dim as oil prices dropped. The Great Depression replaced the Roaring Twenties, and Enid was doubly hit with the Dust Bowl devastating local farmers. Mason membership declined, as people couldn't keep up with their dues, and the countywide lodge split. By the 1940s, the huge temple was larger than the Masons could maintain. Charles Knox, Mason and oilman from Covington, stepped in to buy the building from them and bolster the treasury. Knox was a clever businessman who had started the first gas station in Covington in 1919 and expanded rapidly. His gas was touted as "Knox-less" and superior to other petroleum that might trouble one's engine. He was famed for collectables that he offered with every visit to the gas station, prompting repeat customers to fill up as they worked to complete the collection. The lodge continued in the building, paying rent, but soon even that became too much of a burden, and they moved on. The Knox Building then sat mostly empty for the next four decades.

That's when the first ghost stories began. People noticed that the lights on the fourth floor were shining through the windows all hours of the night. Most people assumed it was a security measure to keep trespassers from sneaking around since their shadows would be broadcast. A few neighborly types would give the building manager a call from time to time to warn about the fourth-floor lights being left on so that he wouldn't be surprised at the end of the month with an enormous electric bill. The manager was thankful for the call, since he was certain that he had shut off all the lights when he left earlier that day.

The calls kept coming, however. Despite the building being locked up, someone would turn the lights on. Suggestions went out of simple absentmindedness, but there were days when no one went into the building at all after the lights were out the night before, and suddenly they were back on by themselves. Looking back on the idea that the lights were on for security, people did see shadows moving around through the upper windows even though the downstairs doors were all securely locked. Police and building managers routinely arrived at the building in the darkest hours of the morning. The locks were secured, but those who ventured inside swore that they could feel someone upstairs and even hear voices or footsteps. Despite thorough searches, no one was ever found.

The obvious answer was that the Knox Building was haunted. It was easy to think with the long corridors and cavernous meeting rooms that some of the Masons who had spent so many evenings there might come back to visit. Hosting a funeral parlor in the lower floors for so many years lent more credence that someone who should have been lain to rest long ago was still around. Even though grown men were quick to scoff at the idea, soon the police and managers who were called in the middle of the night went inside only when there was someone to go with them.

New life came into the building in the 1980s, renovating the building and setting the groundwork that would make it home to the Enid Symphony Orchestra in 2005 in a partnership with Advance Foods. Renovations kept much of the original beauty of the building intact, such as the careful restoration of the Egyptian lobby, modeled like an ancient temple in the style made popular with the recent opening of King Tut's tomb. The Park Avenue Thrift Theatre maintained the proscenium from the Masons' days while adding newly painted murals. Wholly new as the symphony hall, crafted in the vein of the Palace of Versailles with 23-carat gold leaf and eighteenth-century damask fabric on the walls.

With the renovations, there came more stories of something beyond the living dwelling in the halls. At night, just like their forebears, building managers chase phantoms while trying to lock up, certain that they had heard or seen someone but never being able to find a soul. During the day, people frequently hear voices and come into rooms expecting to find a whole conversation going on but instead discover the room is empty. Doors swing open all by themselves, despite having been securely locked.

One legend spread among the musicians that whoever this spirit might be, it is not a fan of music. From time to time, the sheet music on their stands would flutter off or even leap up into the air and cascade across the floor as if someone unseen had smacked it. Douglas Newell, music director for the Enid Symphony Orchestra, had a more mundane explanation. To minimize interference with performances, the renovations had installed a state-of-the-art, totally silent air conditioning system. Things moving or the room suddenly turning cold may not be a ghost so much as the HVAC turning on.

Newell, however, had a strange encounter that he couldn't explain. While working in his office soon after moving in, Newell heard footsteps on the stairs. Few people were in the Knox Building in those days, so he thought he would check to see who was on-site with him. He found a man in blue repairman's coveralls with a nametag, "George," and an elevator company. Newell called out, "Hello!" The man never replied. He just kept stomping down the stairs and sucking on a worn stogie. Newell was flummoxed to see a repairman smoking, something not done in decades. He was even more flummoxed when the sound of the man's footsteps suddenly went quiet.

Hurrying down the stairs, Newell couldn't find any sign of the man. In fact, the doors downstairs were still locked. He decided to call the elevator company from the man's coveralls to see if anyone had an idea what was going on. The company's manager was at a loss: they had no one named George, especially someone who would smoke on a job, but they hadn't even sent anyone to the Knox Building that day. It was a mystery until someone else mentioned seeing "George" and then losing track of him as if he'd vanished. Newell then overheard the explanation: a man named George had served as a facility manager for the building years ago until he had fallen to his death in the elevator shaft.

Though it has been some time since anyone has claimed to have seen George, plenty of people do note a whiff of cigar smoke in the air despite the renovated building being nonsmoking.

14
DEAD MAN'S CAVE

The corner of Third and Oak in Enid has a gruesome and spooky reputation. The reason is twofold.

In 1986, a fourteen-year-old girl went missing. Any time a child goes missing, it is a terrifying thing, but in a town the size of Enid, it is also big news as it is something that doesn't happen often. The '80s was the era of the "latchkey kid," when many kids were left alone while their parents worked. As such, they walked to and from school and found ways to entertain themselves, which often included walking or riding bicycles to their desired destinations. When kids learned of the missing girl, it made them wary to wander too far and to be on high alert if they had to walk anywhere.

A few days had passed since the girl had gone missing when her body was discovered in the storm drainage ditch at Third and Oak. She had been brutally slain and her body purposely dumped there. Police determined the cause of death was stabbing and strangulation.

It was already scary knowing someone had been missing, but finding out she had been murdered was even worse—it meant there were killers on the loose. Walking home from school was even scarier than before. Everyone was hyper-aware of their surroundings and nervous to be alone. One of the murdered girl's schoolmates reported she would walk to her aunt's house a few blocks away every day for lunch. The street to her aunt's house was lined with tall hedges so she would walk down the middle of the street in case anyone was hiding in the bushes.

The formidable entrance to Dead Man's Cave is one of Enid's darkest legends. *Provine's collection.*

Their fears were assuaged two days after the discovery of her body when three boys were arrested in her murder: two brothers, aged fourteen and sixteen, and their fifteen-year-old friend. The friend had apparently planned to kill her by breaking her neck, and he told the sixteen-year-old brother to come to his house to watch. He obliged, and he and the girl were sitting on the couch watching television when the fifteen-year-old boy came up behind her and tried to break her neck, but it only popped. When his plan did not work, he became angry and attacked her with a homemade kama—a blade attached to the end of a long wooden stick. She was stabbed in the neck with the kama and then hit with the stick before both boys had sexual intercourse with her. The brother involved reported to police that he went along with it because he feared his friend and was afraid he would "end up like" her.

The younger brother was not present or involved in the murder, but when he came to the friend's house, they took him to the garage and showed him the girl's body. They had wrapped her in a tent and asked him to help them put her in a wagon. He did, and they wheeled her several blocks away and dumped her in the ditch known as "Dead Man's Cave."

The two older boys were eventually tried as adults, and the youngest one was charged as an accessory and remained in the juvenile system. The older brother was sentenced to forty years and was released in 2001. The friend was sentenced to life in prison, where he remains.

Since the time of that brutal murder, there have been reports of ghostly activity in the area. Two different people on different occasions have reported coming to the stop sign on that corner and having car trouble. One young woman stated she stopped at the stop sign and her car simply died. This is not all that unusual and could easily be a mechanical issue. She popped the hood and got out of her car to investigate when she heard a voice say, "Wait a minute." She looked around to see who was speaking to her. There was no one there, but then she saw an apparition of a young girl walking across the street. She then heard someone say, "It's OK now." She was spooked and quickly got back into her car, which started right up.

Another young woman had a similar account. She had a friend with her in the car, and as they came to that corner, her car started acting up, they saw the apparition of the girl and then her car was fine.

During my research for the *Ghostlahoma* book, I was contacted by a young man asking me if I knew about Dead Man's Cave. I had not heard of it and said as much. He said it was at the corner of Third and Oak. My only knowledge of that area had been about the murder, and I asked if that was what he was talking about. It was not. He relayed the following story.

Several years prior to our conversation, he and a friend had ridden their bikes to the drainage ditch with the intention of exploring it. This was a favorite pastime for Enid boys for many decades, as the storm drains go far under the streets of town. Not long ago, people could travel several blocks through the drains until the city put bars across them to stop it.

The two boys parked their bicycles and wandered into the drain. They walked quite a way into the drain to where there is a ninety-degree turn. As they approached the turn, they heard footsteps. Initially, they were not scared, more curious, as it could have just been other kids doing the same thing they were doing, but they also knew it could be someone they should be wary of. They slowed down, hanging back to see who would emerge from around the corner. The footsteps continued, but when they came around the corner, there was not a body attached to them. What they saw was something else entirely: a big, black mass with red eyes and nothing below the knee.

The terrified boys ran back toward the opening of the drain. The footsteps behind them became faster and faster as if it were chasing them. They got to the opening and scrambled up the hill to get their bikes. There they turned back to see if they were still being followed. The black mass with red eyes was slinking in the shadows just inside the opening of the tunnel, looking up at them. They never went back.

I conduct the Eerie Enid ghost tours, and the corner of Third and Oak is one of the stops. I always told both of these stories and would preface the latter one with the disclaimer that I thought it sounded a little outrageous. One night as I was telling the story, three high school boys on the tour started whispering excitedly to one another. I asked them what they were talking about, and sheepishly one of them looked at the other two and finally said, "We've seen that."

"You have not, you're yanking my braids," I said, smiling.

They were deadly serious and assured me that they had indeed seen the black mass with the red eyes.

Their story bolstered me a bit, and I included it in my telling of the other account on the tour. I said I was not sure if they really had or they were just messing with me until one night a man in his forties slowly raised his hand and said, "I've seen it, too."

There have been at least three or four occasions where men on my tour have claimed to have seen whatever terrifying thing lives in Dead Man's Cave.

One night I had a folklorist on my tour, and she asked me the ages of the people who claimed to see it. I told her it was generally young preteen, teenaged and college boys. She explained the notion of "liminal spaces." According to *In a Liminal Space*, "the word *liminal* comes from the Latin word 'limen,' meaning threshold—any point or place of entering or beginning. A liminal space is the time between the 'what was' and the 'next.' It is a place of transition, a season of waiting, and not knowing."

She explained that the ages I described are all liminal ages—in between being a child and teenager and between being a teenager and an adult—and that often people in liminal ages have experiences other people do not. Liminal spaces can also be physical places, such as theaters, which tend to have an extraordinary amount of ghost stories.

It's a little unsettling to witness a local story become a ghost story and even more so to discover Dead Man's Cave isn't just an urban legend.

Can you brave the cave?

15

GHOSTS OF THE GASLIGHT

On February 22, 1921, the Billings Theater opened its doors to Enid for the first time. Walter S. Billings, sole owner and manager, stated, "Realizing that the greatest need of this community is high-class moving pictures, I have decided to open with this line of entertainment. No expense will be spared in giving the theatrical patrons the highest-class films to be obtained on the market. In addition to these feature productions, I intend to import an orchestra from the east, especially trained to play for entertainments of this character."

Some 2,600 people were estimated to have attended the opening day events. The Billings, said to have been one of the finest appointed playhouses in the entire Southwest, was designed by the world-famous architectural firm of the Boller Brothers. Several offices also took up residence in the theater building. Just months after opening, the theater was sold at a sheriff's sale in late November 1921. Billings was apparently unable to meet the requirements of the mortgage, and his mother, Henrietta, purchased it at the sale.

In March 1922, the name of the theater was changed to the Criterion and remained as such throughout the 1930s. The Criterion managers brought in vaudeville acts in addition to maintaining the movie theater. Just months after becoming the Criterion, the building was ravaged by fire in November 1922. The theater rebuilt, and this time, the owner decided to make it a one-story motion picture playhouse with a seating capacity of 1,200 with apartments taking up the second floor. Henrietta Billings is said to have been

Above: Once the Billings Theater, 221 North Independence is still an address for entertainment in Enid. *Provine's collection.*

Opposite: Who is it that lurks backstage at the Gaslight? *Wilson's collection.*

the one to design the apartments, where she lived until her passing, in the building, from a lingering illness in November 1933.

The building was the Chief Theater from approximately 1940 through 1978, and in 1983, it became the Cinema Twin for a short time. It was purchased by the Gaslight Theatre in 1989.

The Enid Community Theatre troupe was formed in 1966. They originally performed in a building in the 200 block of West Randolph and later took over a warehouse in the 200 block of East Maple, which is now the annex of Leonardo's Children's Museum. In 1989, they had the opportunity to purchase the old Billings building. They renovated it, and the Gaslight Theatre has been their home ever since. Over the one hundred years since the Billings opened its doors, the building has always been a theater, never having gone dark for any significant amount of time.

The Gaslight is one of the most active theaters in the state of Oklahoma. It has shows every month except August and boasts one of the only free Shakespeare in the Park programs in Oklahoma. The theater has an active

QUIET
BACK
STAGE

Narrow stairs lead to the old apartment where footsteps still fall. *Wilson's collection.*

teen program as well as drama camp for elementary school–aged children every summer.

Not only are the living active in the theater but ghosts are as well. It turns out that almost everyone who has spent any amount of time in the theater has at least one ghost story.

I joined the Gaslight Theatre troupe in 1992, shortly after they had taken over the Billings building. I decided to stay late one night to finish painting some set pieces. Everyone had gone home, and I was working on the stage. The auditorium lights were off, illuminated by the working lights over the stage. I had the radio on and was painting away when I got an intense feeling I was being watched. I looked up, thinking someone had come in. There was no one there.

I went back to my work, thinking it must have been my imagination, but I could not shake the feeling of being watched. I looked up toward the tech booth opposite the stage. It was dark, but there appeared to be a shadow up there, looking down at me. I quickly cleaned up and shut things down and went home. The next night at rehearsal, I mentioned what had happened to one of my castmates, and they said, "Oh, yeah, this building is haunted. That happens all the time."

The theater uses the upstairs apartments for storing furniture and props, and it is easily one of the spookiest areas of the entire theater. Many cast and crew members decline to go up there unless they absolutely have to, and most definitely will not go alone. Being in the box office directly beneath them is spooky enough. Everyone who has worked the box office states they have heard footsteps walking around and voices coming from upstairs when they know no one is up there. I heard them myself as I was waiting one night with one of the teen cast members for their parents to pick them up after rehearsal. I had locked everything up and turned everything off. We were sitting on a bench in the box office when footsteps walked across the apartment floor above us.

The tech booth is also the subject of several spooky occurrences. It looks down on the stage so operators can do sound and lights. The booth is a galley-style room, narrow and long like a hallway with doors at both ends. The door at the far end of the room just opens into a small storage area. There is no way into it except through the tech booth. Some people believe in ghosts more than others, and one evening, two men not at all prone to telling ghost stories were working up in the tech booth when they heard a knock coming from the other side of the door at the end of the room. They both knew no one could be in there because they would have had to pass through the room to get there, and no one would even have a reason to be in there. They looked at each other. "Are you gonna look?" one said to the other. "No, are you?" the other one replied. Finally, they opened the door, only to confirm their initial suspicions—no one was there. The knock from the "other side" occurred to another set of castmates, too. They chose not to look.

Many troupe members have stories of seeing the man in the tech booth, standing there and watching. Everyone describes it as unsettling at best. Several of them have also seen someone sitting in the seats in the auditorium—someone not really there.

Several years later, I was hosting a night of ghost stories at the theater. Curtis Tucker and Todd Wheeler from Enid Buzz, a local community social media platform, were with me to livestream it on their page. The three of us were sitting in the auditorium talking while the group wandered the

Even when alone, people say they can hear figures cross the stage or people in the audience. *Wilson's collection.*

building. It was getting late, and Curtis asked if I wanted them to go round everyone up and meet back in the lobby. I told him that I would go backstage and downstairs to the dressing rooms to make sure no one was there. They walked out of the auditorium, and I skipped up the steps to the stage. As I was going behind the curtain, I thought to myself, "I hope someone has something happen so they have a good story." About that time, I heard someone singing on the stage. I knew I was alone in the auditorium, but I stuck my head through the curtain anyway. I was indeed still alone. I didn't want *me* to be the one something happened to!

Another cast member, Mary, reported she had arrived early for a performance one night to make sure she had plenty of time to do her hair and makeup. The back door to the stage was open, and she walked out onto the stage. The stage lights were on, and everything was in its place. She was sure the director was there getting ready for the show. The red velvet curtain was drawn closed so she could not see the auditorium, but she heard a man on the other side of the curtain talking from the seat area right in front of the stage. It sounded as if he were giving directions and moving things around. She peeked through the curtain and said, "Hi, Honey!" to let him know she was there. Then she was overcome with chills. There was no one there. The auditorium was empty, and the lights were off.

She stood there, shocked, for a few moments, when she heard the voice of friend and fellow castmate. She told her what happened as they walked downstairs to the ladies dressing room under the stage. They were talking in the dressing room when they heard the creak of the wooden steps and

Costumes in storage at the Gaslight. *Wilson's collection.*

the thud of a duffle bag on the floor of the men's dressing room on the other side of a thin curtain that separates the two spaces. Her friend jokingly commented loudly, "Wow, someone is here super early," because the men never got there early. No one answered. They both looked at each other, wide-eyed and wary. Mary opened the curtain to have a look. The lights were off, and the room was empty. They went outside to wait on the rest of the cast to get there.

"Clearly someone else was getting ready for a performance, too," Mary said.

One evening, one of the actors was showing her daughter around the theater after they had stricken a set. When they arrived at the downstairs dressing room, her daughter commented she heard someone complaining they were being too loud. There was no one else in the building.

One of the more heartwarming stories about the Gaslight is that of the spot that cannot be lit properly on the stage. Several years ago, *The Best Little Whorehouse in Texas* was in the final stages of production. The show was set to open in two weeks when one of the actors, Todd Smith, passed away from a heart attack. Todd was known for being a ham and commanding a lot of attention with his over-the-top performances. In fact, the theater gives an award named after him every year to the actor or actress who lives up to the Todd factor. As the saying in theater goes, "The show must go on." They found someone to take Todd's place in the show, but ever since Todd passed away, the story goes there is a spot on the stage—the spot he regularly gravitated to—that the light technicians cannot seem to get to light properly. They just call it the Todd Spot. He often gets blamed for things going missing and still pulling pranks.

Yet another common occurrence at the theater is hearing a woman singing or piano music coming from the stage, much like what I experienced. Mind you, there is no piano in the auditorium. During the run of *Rent*, the director was turning everything off and checking the green room to make sure everyone was out so he could lock up. He heard someone singing on the stage. He did not think much of it—*Rent* is a musical, and anyone who has spent any time around musical theater people knows they sing all the time. Since he was ready to go so, the director stuck his head through the curtain to tell whoever it was to come on so he could lock up, and surprise, no one was there.

One day in the dead of summer, two of the Gaslight Teens had spent all morning cleaning the costume loft. There is no airflow up there whatsoever, so it gets very hot. They went downstairs to turn off the lights so they could go have lunch. When they went back upstairs, all the lights were on, and two dresses at the very back of the room—the room with no fans or windows—were swinging around like someone had been yanking on them. They ran downstairs and would not go back up for two days.

Why are so many theaters haunted? Perhaps it is because they are considered liminal spaces, those "in-between spaces" as discussed in the Dead Man's Cave story in this collection. Theaters exist between the real world and a world of make-believe, so this idea certainly fits. Another school of thought is that spirits often attach themselves to physical items, and many community theaters take donations of costumes and furnishing for props, some coming from estates of patrons that have passed away. Still others suggest that theater folk, known to be boisterous and loving to take in a show, are just as lively in the afterlife. In the Gaslight's case, it could be any or all of those reasons.

Or it could be that Henrietta still thinks she owns the place.

16
Old Phillips U

Enid served as the legal and economic center of Garfield County from the beginning and soon grew to be the hub for northeastern Oklahoma. In 1906, several town boosters decided it needed something else: a university. Teaming up with Dr. Ely Vaughn Zollars, former president of Texas Christian University, they drew up a charter for a new Oklahoma Christian University. Citizens were eager to add "college town" to Enid's résumé, and more than $85,000 of funding was raised within one day. More funding flowed in, especially from Pennsylvania oilman and congressman T.W. Phillips, who donated the library. After Phillips's death, the university changed its name in 1912 in his honor.

Phillips University grew by leaps over the twentieth century with new buildings and an athletic program where the "Haymakers" and "Iron Men" football teams defeated even the Texas Longhorns, 10–0 in 1919. In education, the campus hosted a University High School program and established a branch campus in Japan. However, as higher education interests shifted toward larger schools, Phillips was one of the many smaller schools across the nation that closed at the turn of the millennium. In 1998, Northern Oklahoma College came onto the campus, starting a new chapter for learning in Enid. Many signs of the former school remain, including the four columns donated by R.A. Champlain in 1940 from the original façade of the Enid National Bank. Today they still stand alongside University Lake as well as replicas at the Cherokee Strip Regional Heritage Center, each representing one of the four aspects of a holistic life: physical,

The iconic Marshall Building stands as an icon of higher education in Enid. *Provine's collection.*

spiritual, social and intellectual. Phillips also continues in a few spooky stories told in whispers.

Even before the transfer of the campus to NOC, some of the older buildings had already gained legends. The Earl Butts Dormitory, the men's dorm before becoming coed, was rumored to have spirits from an ancient cemetery underneath that would walk through the halls and students' rooms at night. Some students reported feeling weights on their beds like an animal had sprung onto the mattress. After turning on the lights, there was nothing to be found.

The chapel of the Marshall Building is famous for its beautiful windows as well as the sights passersby have witnessed. People have claimed to see shadow figures inside as well as things floating in the air. Sounds, too, trickle through the window of music playing and numerous voices singing. Rushing inside to see who's inside proves the room to be empty.

Another favorite legend of campus is the "Gateway to Hell" on the golf course. The golf course is a regular, run-of-the-mill golf course with no one able to tell where the gateway itself is, unless one considers their years in college or trip around the links to be less than favorable. Yet there are those who maintain that, under the right circumstances, the edge of a bunker glows red and reeks of sulfur.

All the tales pale in comparison to Clay Hall, the old women's dorm. It sits ominously atop a hill on the southwest side of the campus, all alone, separated from the rest of the campus by an expanse of lawn and University Lake with a narrow bridge. The building was closed down even before the end of Phillips University as a fire hazard. Its odd layout makes what looks to be the room at the end of the hall actually a doorway to yet another hall on the other side of the wall. As more regulations for public spaces came into effect, it would indeed have been challenging to get people out quickly in an emergency situation from such a labyrinth. It was said that there were also some asbestos issues, and further water damage inside the once-grand building made it too much of a financial burden for the university to restore. Over time, windows were broken out, boarded up and pried open while the building sat, off-limits but scarcely empty, for years.

Like with most big empty buildings, it became a little foreboding, and stories circulated about its demolition. Other stories spread, too, that the

Pillars still stand on old Phillips University. *Provine's collection.*

Clay Hall has found new life with new residents. *Provine's collection.*

old dormitory is haunted. Some stories are simply far-fetched and silly and made up to make your friends jumpy on a dark night of snooping where they shouldn't. Some stories are rooted in the terrifying truth.

Rumors say a girl died by suicide at old Clay Hall, but this has not been verified. Several stories have, however, been verified about girls being attacked. Folk legends purport it was the actions of a wicked janitor, but that is uncertain, perhaps borrowed from Freddy Krueger movies. These stories go on that his spirit still roamed the empty halls, hunting those teens who dared sneak inside. One of the former Phillips librarians was contacted to see whether they could corroborate any of the urban legends, though a defined historical reason for Clay Hall to be haunted has yet to be determined. That's not to say people haven't had experiences there, however.

A former Phillips student, Ricardo Padilla, recounted what happened to him: "I had always heard stories about Clay Hall. I never really wanted to believe them because, first, I was a skeptic, and second, I never believed a drunk. I spent much of my time around Clay Hall under the influence. Be that as it may, my skepticism rarely wavered. There are two occurrences that stand out in my mind.

"I remember being in Clay Hall one time and hearing about a girl who had committed suicide in one of the rooms. Never one to believe mumbo jumbo, I joined a group of adventurers and wandered aimlessly through the practically condemned building. We happened to enter a room where the suicide supposedly happened. It was a room I believed to be facing south. The windows looked toward a certain section of our school golf course. It was noticeably colder in this room. I just thought through the power of suggestion; maybe I only *believed* it was cooler. Nonetheless, I was quick to hurry myself out of the room.

"The second time I experienced weirdness involving Clay Hall, I was walking home from a house party. I was alone. I happened to look up and saw a figure looking at me from about the same area I had previously been—the room that allegedly housed the suicide victim. I didn't believe my eyes at first, so I glanced again. It almost seemed as if I could make out a girl with long hair with a strange glow and eyes that followed me. I knew this was impossible. There was no way I could see any features, especially eyes, at the distance I was. But I did. So, I did what most people I know would do: I freaked out and started sprinting toward the dorms as fast as I could. Still to this day, I occasionally dream about this place. It spooks me, and I'm not usually spooked."

One Enid resident reported she and her cousins would accompany their parents to fish at the lake at the bottom of the hill, and they would run off to play around Clay Hall. She recounted how they would look in the windows and could see streamers from a bygone party still hanging. If they watched long enough, the streamers would begin to blow as if a fan were blowing on them. Even scarier, she said they would sometimes hear screaming coming from inside the building.

There are several reports of seeing a woman watching from the upper windows, even moving from floor to floor in the blink of an eye. More stories describe shadowy figures watching people as they passed by. People who ventured inside tell of seeing a ball of light move through the wall and hearing disembodied sounds coming from closed-off areas of the dormitory. Some even recorded the singing of an unseen woman, accompanied by the sounds of a piano even though no instrument was present.

Clay Hall has since been renovated into a senior apartment complex, giving the old building a new role and new residents. One of the contractors working on the renovation claimed they had several strange things happen while they were working on the building. Even after reopening, the strange things continue. A current resident reported objects that unexplainably fall, doors open on their own and lights that were turned off coming on. A gentleman resident also relayed that, when he lived there, he would often be awakened at night by knocks on his doors or walls. He also witnessed doors opening and closing on their own. He reported hearing a young girl asking for her mother. Ultimately, he decided to move.

17
BARSIDE TALES

The oldest bar in town, open since 1948, is the Frisco Bar located at 608 North Independence. "Frisco" had long been a name in Enid, one of the main lines running through town that made Enid the rail hub of the entire region. The Frisco Hotel once served clients a bit farther on Independence, near the St. Louis–San Francisco depot that was one of many on the complex of railyards north of downtown.

The Frisco Bar was originally down the street from its current location, but that building is no longer there. The current building was a machine shop downstairs with a brothel upstairs. The Frisco is famous for its ice-cold beer, but there are chilly spirits of another kind there, too.

A massive collection of beer bottles and cans lines the upper walls of the bar. One evening, the owner, Jim O'Neill, was standing behind the bar visiting with one of the customers when *one* beer bottle came flying several feet away from the shelf and nearly hit the customer at the bar. Now, keep in mind that these cans and bottles are nestled quite close together on these shelves in tiers, but not a single other one of them was disturbed by the one that seemingly propelled itself off the shelf.

The incident of the flying can is hardly the only strange activity of identified moving objects. A picture has also fallen off the wall and to the floor, and again, not one can or bottle was disturbed. O'Neill and other employees have witnessed the water faucet at the sink behind the bar coming on by itself as well.

For more than three-quarters of a decade, the Frisco Bar has been an Enid mainstay. *Provine's collection.*

They say the Frisco ghost is to blame for the flying objects and random water running. In the early morning hours one day, O'Neill and another man were in the bar. O'Neill had just returned from picking up the newspaper from the front sidewalk when his friend asked, "Didn't you lock that back door?"

O'Neill assured him he had.

The man told him he had heard it open and said, "Someone just walked up that ramp to the men's room."

O'Neill wasn't too worried about it. "That's just the ghost."

He reported that people often hear the back door open, and when they look to see who's coming, they witness a black figure walking up the ramp toward the men's room. Though the origins of the ghost are unknown, O'Neill and some of the others are used to it by now. Some won't readily admit to believing in it but will certainly clean up as quickly as they can when they're there alone.

Yet the Frisco isn't the only haunted place to get a drink in town. The Spot, located at 417 North Grand, is a popular bar a few blocks from downtown Enid. In 1935, the building housed a grocery store that remained into the 1960s. In 1968, it became Tydings Wholesale, a tobacco company that was there until 1980 when it became B&B Manufacturing. In 1982, Hunt's Furniture & Appliances moved in, and then from 1983 to 2015, it was the home of the AmVets office. It has since been one of the hottest night spots in Enid with regular live music, pool tables, pinball, darts and a full liquor bar.

In 2019, the bar owner announced on Facebook, "I think my bar is haunted."

One of the first things that prompted the announcement was when the bar staff heard a gunshot inside the building. The bar had closed, the patrons had all left and the staff was cleaning and restocking. The owner was behind the bar when a gunshot rang out. He instinctively hit the floor and drew his own gun. He was certain someone was shooting up the place. After a moment, he went to investigate and discovered there was only staff in the bar, all the doors were locked and all the windows were fully intact. There was no explanation or evidence of a gun being shot in the building.

The staff, too, began noticing odd things happening on a regular basis. Each person who works there has different stories, which continue to rack up.

One of the bartenders stated that she had restocked the cooler with beer and was working behind the bar when the doorman told her he was going to take out the trash. When he came back in, she scolded him, saying, "Look, if you wanted a beer, I could have gotten you one. You didn't need to take one right out of the front of the cooler I just stocked."

He looked at her, confused, and told her he had not taken a beer. He went on to say that he does not even drink beer. Yet there was a bottle missing right from the front row of newly stocked beers. They both looked all around and never found an errant bottle. It was as if it had just disappeared into thin air.

The same bartender relayed that there was a spot where the Crown Royal bottle usually sat and that no matter how many times the bottle was placed in its spot, it would move.

There have been reports of bottle caps being thrown but no one there to throw them and even disembodied voices. One night during their closing routine, the owner made a comment outside the closed ladies room door, and he heard a female voice respond, "I'll be right out." He then noticed that all his female staff were in the bar, not in the restroom. He waited a moment and had one of the girls check the bathroom in case there might be a leftover customer. No one was inside.

There are cameras throughout the bar so whoever is working the door can see what is happening from their monitors. One night after the bar had closed, the doorman noticed a chair was pulled away from one of the tables. They stepped out into the bar to put it back and discovered it was right where it was supposed to be, pushed under the table. Another look at the monitor showed it was still pulled out. Another time, the staff were all leaving after closing, and one of them forgot something, so they went back into the bar with him and discovered a chair had been pulled out into the middle of the floor in the short time it had taken them to walk out and walk back in.

After several odd occurrences, they had a paranormal investigation team come spend some time there. Some of the investigators were in the front part of the building attempting to collect EMF readings or any other evidence they could get. One of the bar staff was in the back room with a Ouija board, but after not getting much response, they moved out where the chairs were. There they asked the Ouija board what the name of the ghost haunting the bar was. It spelled out "Al," that he was seven years old and that he had died there. While she was asking the questions, one of the investigators was recording audio. When she played it back as soon as they were done asking questions, a voice on recorder said "Al" at the same time the board was spelling out the name.

Unexplained events continued after the official investigation. On another occasion, the inner door was closed, and it began shaking and rattling violently before it suddenly stopped. They also report seeing solid, deliberately moving balls of light on the cameras. Oftentimes after they've finished cleaning, and everyone is sitting down before leaving for the night, they will all hear noises coming from the restroom area. One day, one of the girls was hanging up some decorative signs. She laid one on the bathroom sink and went to get a hammer and nail, and when she returned, the sign was gone. It has never been found.

One of the bartenders had lost someone very special to her, and on the anniversary of their passing, she was hanging out after the bar closed. The jukebox came on and played the song that bartender had had with the friend she had lost. They all looked at each other and inquired if anyone had played it. No one had.

The bar was closed for a private party one evening. The partygoers had been conversing and playing pool when someone called everyone up to the bar to do shots together. Heading over to the bar, someone left a stack of quarters on one of the tables, not thinking anything of them. They did their celebratory shots and talked for a few minutes before returning to the table, where they found the quarters that had been stacked were now arranged in an X on the table, each one standing up on its edge! Every attendee of the party had been at the bar.

So, is it spirits or the spirits causing the chaos at the Spot? With its density of crazy things happening, it could likely be one of the most haunted spots in town.

18

Morbid

The Haunted Museum

After working for years with classic spook houses like Enid's Nightmare Warehouse, Tracy Ullrich decided he wanted to treat people to a completely different kind of scare. Rather than the shock of a jump scare with an actor in costume leaping out amid strobe lights, he envisioned a deeper, penetrating horror simply by presenting cursed or strange objects and telling their stories. Ullrich had already built up a collection of spooky artifacts from his own fascination with the macabre. Putting them in a museum would give others a chance to experience one-of-a-kind thrills.

Besides, he needed them out of his house before anything else weird happened to his family. Strange things seemed to happen when he brought certain objects into his house, such as the time he woke up in a sobbing fit convinced that demons were prowling the room. Ullrich moved that certain haunted doll out of his house, and things got better. Now everyone has a chance at nightmares themselves.

The resulting Morbid: the Haunted Museum presents visitors the chance to see. Ullrich states that he has more than five hundred objects in the collection, which is always growing. This keeps exhibits rotating so that no two visits to the museum are the same while also giving a chance for special collections in themed rooms. Ullrich says he likes to play music, especially gothic organ music, not only to set ambience but also to keep himself from getting too spooked when something makes a sound without rational explanation. Sometimes the jolly chimp doll likes to clap its cymbals despite the mechanism inside being broken years ago.

Many of the objects aren't necessarily possessed themselves but feature a connection to the macabre. Exhibits in the front of the museum, before things start getting really spooky, include wooden carvings of ancient Mesopotamian deities, the Annunaki; Indigenous artifacts from rituals comforting the dying; and papers from Poveglia, the island hospital outside Venice where plague victims were exiled by the thousands. Near-mint embalming machines from the C.M. Sorensen Co., well over a century old, stand seemingly innocent until the story is revealed how it could also be used as dental anesthesia, perhaps even on the same patient whose tooth infection spread. A pair of sick call boxes with kits for Catholic last rites rest across from each other with crosses, holy water bottles and plates for communion. One is pristine; the other is well used, with tarnished marks on the crucifix showing the prints where thumbs and hands held it in their final moments.

Muderobilia makes up a good portion of the Haunted Museum. Hundreds of letters from famous serial killers cover entire walls along with information detailing the murderers who wrote them. The range of murderers is broad, from the satanic Caius Veiovis who bears tattoos and horns through body-modification to the sadistic Tool Box Killers Lawrence Bittaker and Roy Lewis Norris, to grandmotherly Dorothea Puente, who poisoned pensioners in her boardinghouse. Some of the letters are written in blood mixed with ink, giving a rust color to the scrawled words along with bloody thumbprints to show it is their own.

For every item that isn't ghostly, such as an unused child's coffin holding up the Chuckles the clown doll, there is something terrifyingly spooky, such as the *well-used* child's casket. This polished wooden box was used as a display for funerals or wakes of children, who, once the viewings were over, would then be transferred to a simpler box for final burial. Impressions in the padding under the shiny cloth lining show where untold numbers of little heads and shoulders rested. Something about it seems to trigger the EMF reader in response to questions, and guests who come close say they hear pained breathing.

The Haunted Museum's collection holds classic haunted artifacts such as paintings, a wedding veil carefully done up in a shadow box and pump organs where a shadowy man appears in the mirror standing behind the player. While some collections may tout one dybbuk box (a container where a demon is entrapped during an exorcism), this museum has so many that only a fraction are on display at a time. Many are plain locked wooden boxes, others are tied with cords and one even offers a darkened glass portal where a peeking face has been photographed. Several boxes come from the estate of a collector who worked with exorcists and used his barn to store the boxes. After the collector passed, the boxes were sold off or given away, always with the warning that strange things may happen, like humanoid shadows moving without a person to make them, handprints where no one had been and knocking sounds from rooms empty other than the boxes. Ullrich was told they seem to become more active when they're given attention, making something of an experiment out of the museum itself.

One of the stars of the Haunted Museum is the little doll Emeraldine. She has curly brown hair, a pretty white dress and a leather band with an emerald ring tied around her torso. When Ullrich bought the doll, the legend was that she belonged to a witch who would wear the ring while she danced with the doll. The doll, too, would move on her own to dance to her favorite song, Bobby Day's "Over and Over." Today the doll rests inside an old combination television/record player stand and reacts to an EMF meter while the song plays. Several guests have had odd reactions themselves. As Ullrich was putting up the doll during a tour, one man shouted at him not to close the stand doors. He shouted, "She doesn't like it!" After fidgeting erratically, the man stormed out and was later found weeping, not knowing what had come over him. Another time, a young lady screamed at her boyfriend when he softly kept singing "Over and Over," something she had never done before but said the doll wanted him to stop.

One of the many dolls said to move and react on its own at the Haunted Museum. *Provine's collection.*

Emeraldine is hardly the only spooky doll in the collection. Charlotte, pictured, reacts to children, a surprise that came to Ullrich after setting a motion-sensor in her dress. If the doll is shaken or tapped, the sensor will begin flashing colorful lights. Lights going off when no one is near could be explained through micro-earthquakes or a heavily stamped foot, if not for the coincidence of going off only when kids were around. Ullrich said he first noted the strange activity from the doll whenever his son came through the front door at home. It wouldn't light up for anyone else entering, just the boy. Charlotte soon found a place up front in the museum, welcoming kids. Other dolls require a close watch, such as the pair of sock monkeys who seem to find their way back to each other no matter where they are set apart.

Yet none of the dolls carry the international fame of the world's most haunted jack-in-the-box. It was once sold on an online auction with a poem the seller said the jack-in-the-box said to her in a dream,

I stand around one foot tall
Don't fool with me or you might die
Where I come from, no one knows
But wherever I go, more fear grows
Treat me well and you will see
What old Jack can do for thee.

When Ullrich bought the jack-in-the-box, it arrived by mail in a cloud of eeriness. The mailman hand-delivered it rather than setting it by the door so that he could ask what it was. Despite a truck full of other boxes, this was the only one that made him unsettled. Ullrich didn't think too much about it until someone else stopped in, pointed at the box in the middle of other boxes in his office, and asked what was giving him such a bad feeling. He said he could almost picture the jack's striped face. When a shadowy figure began appearing on the walls, Ullrich packed up the jack-in-the-box to move it to a safer location surrounded by salt and sage.

Visitors ought not touch objects or photograph them in case it creates a connection that allows the spirit to travel beyond the museum. This is a horror that creeps over visitors and, according to some guests, may very well follow them home.

19
Murder House

In 1984, one of the grisliest murders in Enid's history occurred when a prominent businessman we'll call "Mr. Smith" was attacked and brutally murdered in his home.

On the evening of the murder, Mr. Smith had two young male guests with him. They were in the bedroom watching a movie when someone rang the doorbell. Smith went to answer the door. When he opened it, he was rushed by two men who stabbed him repeatedly in the entryway of his home.

One of the attackers went to deal with the other two men. As one of the guests was trying frantically to get out of the doors that led outside from the bedroom, he was grabbed and also brutally stabbed to death. The police later discovered three inches of a filet knife broken off inside the man's brain, yet the murderer had continued stabbing him even after the blow to the brain had already killed him.

During the melee, the third man seemed to have disappeared. The two cold-blooded killers searched the house, leaving bloody footprints, but could not locate him anywhere. What they didn't know was that in the bedroom, near the back wall, was a small cabinet that was not easily seen. The survivor had quietly slipped into it and hid there, sweating and terrified, as he could hear his assailants looking for him, asking each other where he could have gone. He stayed silent, cooped in a tiny cabinet for some five or six hours.

The next morning, when he was confident he was alone, he left his cramped hiding place and called the police. The police arrived and witnessed one of the most brutal scenes in Enid's history. The light-colored carpet now oozed crimson. Police of course questioned the third man; they found it hard to believe with all the blood and mess that he had gone unscathed. He told them he had hidden in the cabinet to escape the predators. They wanted to see it, so he showed them, but they immediately disbelieved it. The cabinet was both incredibly narrow and not very tall and unfathomable how a grown man, small or not, could have gotten in it. The police asked him how he could have possibly gotten in there, let alone hide for so long. He placed his foot on the small table near the cabinet and boosted himself into the small space once again. Sure enough, they were able to later find a footprint in the back of the cabinet, corroborating the man's story.

After thirteen hours at the bloody crime scene, the police had no hard evidence against anyone, though they had an idea of who it was. There were three people who had been in the park adjacent to the house, and they were able to give physical descriptions of the attackers and the car they arrived in. It was not lost on the police that the attackers were seen wearing gloves yet parked a yellow Camaro right in front of the house. Without actual evidence, though, it would be difficult to close the case.

Upon going through the house, the police found a closet full of explicit videos. The blue movie the victims had been watching was still playing on a constant loop in the bedroom from the time of the murders. When police reviewed the movie, the medical examiner made a comment that one of the acts was "medically impossible." Explicit pictures were found as well, though no one outside of the police department has ever seen them.

The investigator decided the best way to arrest to the killers would be to find a woman they were close to—the best way to get to a man, after all, is through a woman. They located someone they knew to be friendly with one of the suspects and approached her. She agreed to help them and began calling, visiting and talking at length with the suspect, all the while with the police listening. Over the weeks she spoke with the man, he confessed to her that he'd killed a man in California. He had been hitchhiking when a man picked him up. The driver made a sexual advance toward him, so he beat him in the head with a wrench until he was dead and left his body in the trees. He killed another man in Georgia, leaving the body to rot in the swamp. But he never spoke of the Enid murders.

The woman eventually decided to leave the state, but when she did, she decided to take the investigator's tape recorder with her. They had no way to reach her or get her back, so the investigator approached her sister and told her that if the woman did not return to Oklahoma, he would have to file embezzlement charges against her for taking his tape recorder. Not wanting trouble with the police, the informant returned to Oklahoma. They reminded her that she'd agreed to help them and expected her to do just that. She said, "OK, let's do this," and they once again set out to get a confession out of the suspect.

Some days later, the woman contacted the police to let them know the suspect wanted to take her out to the Gloss Mountains, the same remote range of mesas out in northwestern Oklahoma where outlaws like Dick Yeager hid out nearly a century before. The police devised a plan to follow and listen, worried that her safety might be in jeopardy. Out in the middle of nowhere, there were not many close places for the police to conceal themselves and get to her in time if anything untoward were to happen. During the trek to the Gloss Mountains, the suspect spilled his guts about the Enid murders, and the police were able to get the entire confession on tape thanks to the informant. He was later sentenced to life in prison, where he remains.

The man never testified in Oklahoma about the second man involved in the killings; he had moved on to Texas. He met a woman with had an ex-boyfriend who owned a jewelry store, and she thought they could rob it. They went to his house to confront him and demand loot. The killer had fashioned a ten-pound samurai sword, and when the store owner turned on him, he split him from the shoulder to the navel and then ran the sword through the man's brain when he fell to the ground.

His partner from the Enid murder later testified about his involvement in the Oklahoma killings when the second man went to trial in Texas for the slaying of the jewelry store owner. The police were able to obtain the transcripts of that trial and wanted to use them to bring action against the second man in Oklahoma, but the victim's family was not interested in opening up old wounds or having to deal with such a high-profile case anymore. It was over for them, and that's how they wanted it to stay. Even though the second man was never brought to trial in Oklahoma, he was eventually executed in Texas.

Something particularly odd about this story is that there is only one person left who can tell us what happened that night, and he is in prison. His defense attorney passed away, as has the houseguest who hid in the cabinet, and the second man involved in the killings has been executed. Despite the confession and conviction, the reason for the murder of Mr. Smith has never been discovered. There has been much speculation, from unpaid drug debts to bribery. The drug theory does not carry much weight considering Mr. Smith was financially stable, and it is unlikely he would have owed anyone money for marijuana. Another school of thought is that Mr. Smith sometimes met and entertained young men after they got out of jail. It was said he would spend some time with them and then give them some money to help them leave town. As such, these people would not be around to spread rumors or tell stories in town, so it was a good arrangement. It is thought perhaps the killer had been one of these men, and he had been trying to muscle more money out of Mr. Smith but was not getting the compliance he demanded.

After the murders, the family of the victim took over the house and eventually lived there for several years until another family bought it. In the early 2000s, the Eerie Enid paranormal investigation team was contacted by a teenaged boy that told them, "I think my house is haunted." His mother worked out of town and was gone a lot, and his father no longer lived in the house, so the boy was there on his own quite often. With such freedom, his house was the house where all his friends crashed, and they eventually started a band without having to worry about adults complaining of noise. There was never a shortage of teen boys in the house, and several of them told stories of strange things. They said that they would see someone in the kitchen, realize no one should have been, and then go to investigate and find no one there. Even when alone in the house, the boy who contacted the team would hear noises as if someone else was moving around. It was a string of common haunted house stories.

As the teens continued to relay the happenings at the house, they stated what disturbed them most was that they would often be awakened by someone playing with their hair or touching their faces. When they sat up and looked around, there was never a living soul to be found.

Even before visiting the house, investigators asked its location so they could do historical research about why there might be a reason for the haunting. The teen said, "Oh, you probably know the house—it's the Smith house." Suddenly things very quickly made sense.

Disclaimer: The preceding story is true, and the facts are accurate. I was able to interview the police investigator who worked this case. I knew the occupant of the house and was able to tour the house with the investigator. This story has been one told in my hometown since it happened when I was a child, so it was of course fascinating for me to be able to actually learn about it from the people who knew the most about it. I have, however, changed the name of the victim and not mentioned the names of the murderers. People in my town will know the story anyway, but I wanted to respect the family and not bring attention to the criminal or danger on myself by putting his name in a book.

20

Devil House

Shirley was so excited. Her little family was finally moving from their tiny, cramped studio apartment into a roomy two-bedroom house with a yard for her one-year-old daughter to play in. It was an older home, and they had a lot of cleaning up to do to make it habitable, but that did not dampen their spirits.

Within just weeks of moving in, odd things started happening. At first it was just small things. A ceramic Trojan horse was moved from the TV cabinet to the fireplace mantel. The heavy leather recliner would be turned to face the corner—a chair so heavy it was difficult to move in any direction. Often, drawn shades would be opened, and opened shades would be drawn shut. There were times Shirley experienced strange and creepy feelings she could not explain, but they were young and inexperienced and didn't take things too seriously. They laughed it off and joked that they probably had a poltergeist.

Things started to escalate, and they were no longer laughing. One evening, Shirley went into the kitchen and was shocked to find all the cabinet doors and drawers hanging open. The forks and knives were stuck in the ceiling—dangling there ready to fall on any individual wandering in. It was no longer funny. The "feelings" became foreboding, and she was apprehensive about being alone in the house. However, once a week her husband worked out of town, leaving her alone in the house and as the sole protector of the baby. She had to lay her fears and anxieties aside and shelter the baby from any possible harm.

One night, around 3:00 a.m., Shirley was sleeping soundly when she was abruptly awakened. She found herself dragged halfway off the bed. She wasn't aware when it was happening but suddenly found herself partially on the floor. Trembling, she jumped up to check on the baby. Shirley's bedroom door was shut, and the lights were on. Upon opening the door, she found all the lights in the house were on. All the doors, cabinets and drawers were flung open. The front and back door were wide open, and their St. Bernard was cowering under the dining table, whimpering.

She ran to the baby, scooped her from her crib, grabbed her diaper bag and headed for the car. They found a well-lit parking lot and spent the night there. After returning home the next day, she informed her husband of the events that had transpired the previous evening. Refusing to return to the house, they hurriedly found another house and moved.

Eighteen years later, Shirley was an employment counselor doing an intake on a new client. Seeing his address, she mentioned she had lived in that house at one time. He asked, "Anything weird ever happen to you there?"

Shirley and her client exchanged stories about the house, and she found that he had been having the same strange things going on there nearly twenty years later.

Shirley is my mother, and I was that baby. I always thought this was a great example of a haunted house since two completely unrelated people had things happen there, so I frequently relayed this story to friends during ghost story sessions. One evening I was telling the story to my friend who worked at a local pharmacy, and when I mentioned the address, he became white as a ghost himself and started pacing around the room, incredulous. He said to me, "We used to deliver medicine to a lady that lived there, and we always thought she was crazy because she was always going on about how the devil lived in her house!"

The house is a rental and is available often.

21

Granny's House

The big Queen Anne–style house on West Broadway was built in 1910 and changed hands a few times before the Johnson family acquired it in 1956. At that time, Dr. and Mrs. Howard Johnson and their daughter, Dr. Jeanne Johnson, lived in the home. They had another daughter, Jayne, Jeanne's identical twin, who was married and had a family. Though living in her own home, she and her family spent much of their time at her parents'.

Dr. Johnson was the first of the family to pass away, followed by Jeanne, and then Mrs. Johnson, whom the family called "Granny." Among the family, the house is known as "Granny's House." Jayne was the only survivor of Dr. Johnson's immediate family for many years, but that did not mean that the old house was empty. Several of the family members claim to have heard and seen things in the house over the years that cannot be explained, such as footsteps, voices and doors banging.

It was a tradition for the whole family to spend the night at Granny's House on Christmas Eve. One cold, snowy Christmas Eve, the little boys were awakened by a bump in the night. They went to investigate, and they saw Santa Claus on the landing! The next morning, there was a note in one of the boys' stockings telling him presents from Santa were at his house. A skeptic would think it was just one of the grown-ups pretending to be Santa and the boys, in their drowsy state, just didn't recognize them. That would be a likely explanation. However, none of the adults has ever admitted to it in over twenty years, not even among themselves in private conversations. Not only have they not admitted to it, but they have all flat-out denied it.

Jayne was my step-grandmother. In the late fall of 1996, my husband and I moved into the home after she inherited it. There were still some of the original antique furnishings that we used in the house and a big portrait of Dr. Johnson hanging on the dining room wall. We felt it only proper and respectful to leave the portrait there, as it had been his house, after all. We were expecting a new baby in the spring, and we were excited to begin our family in this grand old home. When we first moved in, we heard doors banging and such coming from upstairs quite frequently; then after a while it stopped. We assumed it was Aunt Jeanne's ghost, and once she realized we were family, she liked us and stopped trying to scare us.

The baby's room was upstairs directly across from our room. Sometimes at night, footsteps would be heard over the baby monitor. I would frantically run to check on the baby only to find everything as it should be.

As it is when a newborn comes home, the mother doesn't get a lot of sleep. One morning I woke up and realized that I had slept through the entire night. At first, I was excited to think that my baby was finally starting to sleep through the night, but then I became worried. I quickly went to check on things; the baby was fine and sleeping soundly. I returned to my room and inspected the baby monitor. It was turned off. Neither my husband nor I ever turned off the baby monitor. We often wondered if perhaps Aunt Jeanne was watching over us and knew that, as a new mom, I was tired and needed rest, so she turned the monitor off to let me sleep.

Jayne, Jeanne's twin, had moved down the street with my parents, where our family visited them frequently. My daughter came to know her as "Nana Jayne." When our second daughter came along, we moved our oldest from the nursery into the room next to ours, Jeanne's old room. One summer day when the baby was about eighteen months old, she was sitting on the bed in her room. The child looked up at the doorway as if someone had just walked into the room and said, "Hi. Hi, Nana Jayne."

There was no one there. The hair on my neck stood up, and my skin crawled because I knew who she had seen. Jeanne and Jayne were identical twins, and if the child had seen Jeanne, she would assume it was Jayne, not knowing any difference since Jeanne had passed away long before any of us had a chance to meet her.

A few years later, the same child woke up in the night claiming that someone had sat on her bed and woke her up. She didn't want to sleep in there anymore. Bad dreams haunted her, and all she would say about them was that a scary man was at the bottom of the stairs.

One night, I awoke to the sound of sobbing. I got up and checked on all the kids, only to find them sleeping soundly. I walked through the entire house and couldn't find where the crying was coming from. There were drive-through restaurants on either side of the house, and I thought perhaps voices from the intercoms were carrying. I went out the front door—nothing. I went out the back door—nothing. I woke my husband and made him look with me. He could not hear it and thought I was crazy. After I looked everywhere, I finally gave up and went back to bed. But I could still hear those sobs. It bothered me for about an hour before I finally went back to sleep. When I woke up again a couple of hours later, the crying had stopped.

Later, when I questioned the family about whether they'd ever experienced the sobs, they told me that Jeanne had a fiancé who had been killed in a car accident. She spent a significant amount of time sobbing over him.

When we had been living there about six years, the family decided they had to sell it and we had to move out. We moved across town, and my daughter's bad dreams stopped. For a period of about a year, the house was unoccupied, and eventually we offered to buy the old house. We decided that while the house was empty, we would remodel before moving back in.

Right before we were going to move back in, my mother asked me about having a séance there. I said absolutely not, as I didn't want to stir anything up, but I asked her why she thought about it. She then relayed that, while my uncle was in the house doing some repair work, he confided in my mother that he heard noises and voices upstairs. When he went upstairs to confront whoever was in the house, no one was there. Another evening, my mother had gone there to get something out of the house, and she heard banging upstairs. She yelled, "It's just me—I'll be gone in a minute." The banging stopped. The house had been empty the whole time.

Another time, a friend of the family took her son and her boyfriend to the house to look at it with her. It was the middle of summer in Oklahoma, which translates to being deadly still and hot in the house. When they approached the landing on the second floor, the prisms on the ceiling light fixture began shaking violently. Now, I had lived in this house for years and never witnessed anything like that, even when the adjacent attic fan was on. There was no wind at all this day. The two grown men turned and ran out of the house. Our friend spoke out loud and told the house she was a friend. The shaking stopped. Still, she reported that she felt like it was not necessarily friendly.

One night, I had to go into the house myself to get something. I was overwhelmed by an uneasy feeling as I went up the stairs. I had lived in this house for a long time, and I loved it, so I was not normally scared there, but this night was different. When I came the room to get what I had come after, I was consumed with this "get the hell outta here" feeling. I literally ran out of the house.

So, with these rather unnerving things taking place since the house had become empty, I was a little nervous about moving my children back into it. I contacted a paranormal investigation team to come check it out. What they found was very interesting, to say the least. During the time the house was unoccupied, Jayne had passed away, so now all of the original Johnson family was gone. When the investigative team was there, they recorded a woman's voice saying "Hello" in the same exact manner as Jayne always said it. It was so much like her voice that it brought several family members to tears when they heard the recording.

The recording also had a heartbeat that preceded the voice. They tried to re-create recording a heartbeat and were not successful. The recording was sent to a cardiologist to analyze. The doctor told them it was the heartbeat of someone with congestive heart failure, which Jayne had.

The team was able to validate that the house was possibly haunted but did not feel there was anything particularly menacing in it. However, when I returned to my house across town after the investigation that night, I had something odd happen. No one was home, and I went in the front door and directly to the back door to let the dog out. When he came back, he followed me into the living room, where I lay down on the couch. Our dog, Slurpie, was a big boxer. He stood in front of me and looked past me at something behind me; the hair on his back bristled up, and he began to bark angrily. I tried to get his attention, but he ignored me. I called his name a few times, but he was focused on something behind me, barking and snarling. I finally grabbed his collar on both sides, trying to get him to look at me, but he wouldn't. He was clearly upset about something, and frankly, I was too scared to look behind me to see what it was. Then he suddenly stopped and turned away. All I know is that from that day forward, whatever was unfriendly at the big Broadway house was gone. I think it followed me home, freaked my dog out and went on its way.

We moved back into the house on Broadway a few months later, and it seemed to us that the negative feelings were indeed gone. Things went well, and there were no odd occurrences. We chalked it up to the house being happy we were back home. Then one night, I was in my room putting away laundry when my oldest daughter, the one who had had all the prior experiences, yelled, "What?"

"What, what?" I replied.

She came walking into my room and said, "You called me, what did you want?"

I had not called her, but she said she clearly heard me call her name.

Another night, my husband went in to read her a bedtime story. I went to bed and fell asleep. Later that night, my husband frantically woke me up. He was obviously flustered, and I asked him what the matter was. He had fallen asleep in our daughter's room and was awakened by my voice whispering to him, "Marty, get up and come to bed." He said he heard it a couple of times, but when he got up, I was not there. He found me sound asleep in our bed even though he swore it was my voice.

My grandmother came to my house every morning to care for my children while I worked. I was in the upstairs bathroom one morning doing my hair when I heard her call my name from the bottom of the stairs. I yelled back, "What?" She didn't answer, and I figured it wasn't that important. I finished getting ready and went downstairs. She was coming out of the kitchen, and I asked her what she had hollered at me about. She looked at me and said, "I just walked in the back door. I didn't holler at you."

I became a little frightened that three different people in my house had heard their names called by a familiar voice that was not any of us in the house doing it. Other than that, there were no other experiences, and we ended up only living there a year and a half before we moved into my husband's family home.

My cousin took over the old Johnson family house. When they were getting ready to move in, she asked me not to tell her husband about any of it because she didn't think he would stay there. But if things are still happening, it's more than likely just her family keeping things interesting. I did tell her it might be a good idea to leave that portrait of Dr. Johnson on that dining room wall, just in case.

A few years later, the house was sold to some friends of the family who happened to have young children. They continue to have regular ghostly experiences at Granny's House.

22
The Hero of Government Springs Park

The five natural springs that spout in today's Government Springs Park were a destination long before Enid was founded. Native Americans stopped there to drink from the cool water, renowned as a great source of health to rival those at Medicine Park and Sulfur. In later generations, the cowboys of the Chisholm Trail drove untold millions of cattle through what would become Enid, stopping to water at Government Springs, the first big rest after leaving Bison Springs near present-day Bison to the south. They would then move on northward to the ford at Skeleton Creek, where the ranch and stagecoach station would later be established. Today those past visitors are commemorated with artwork of black metal silhouettes that stand watch over the springs today.

Following the land run, the springs were a major source of water for the settlers, even after many of them dug their own wells. No one could claim the land for their own by city mandate, making the water accessible to all. One enterprising nineteen-year-old, Richard Messall, was too young for his own claim, but within two days of his parents staking in Enid, he had set up a business selling bottled spring water. The resulting Enid Soda and Mineral Water Company was the first manufacturing firm in town. Dr. G.A. Boyle took interest in the healing aspects of the mineral water and set up the Enid Springs Sanitarium nearby. It grew and was later donated to become the start of St. Mary's Hospital.

Government Springs Park became one of the first official recreational areas in town in 1911, circling the natural lagoon made by the spring water

Government Springs Park still shows off the WPA construction beautifying the springs. *Provine's collection.*

Healthy water encouraged founding a sanitarium, which would later evolve into the hospital that would become St. Mary's. *Courtesy of Cherokee Strip Regional Heritage Center.*

spilling down the slopes. This was a place for boating, fishing and swimming before the cleaner municipal pool was established, piping in the chilly spring water. Boggy Creek flowed nearby, often backing up and flooding into the park, so WPA workers corrected the problem with a deep channel and riprapping slopes that maintained the two. Workers also built the sloping concrete bridge that has been a hallmark of photos for the park for nearly a century. Groundwater pollutants eventually made the springs unfit for human drinking, but the park is still enjoyed by thousands every year with outdoor symphony performances and the annual Shakespeare in the Park.

January 1963 saw a terrible tragedy at the park. It had been bitterly cold the week before, warmed up, and then temperatures dropped again to one and two degrees above zero the two nights before. The lake iced over, so nine-year-old Robert Lee Owens and his seven-year-old friend Julius Franklin went out to "ice skate" across it. While the ice at the edges was thick, the middle of the water had only a thin layer on top. It cracked and then gave way under Franklin, who couldn't swim. Owens could not swim either, but he could not stand by and let his friend drown. He slid across the ice trying to help until he, too, fell into the freezing water. Owens pushed Franklin out, who cried for help when Owens went under the ice. Their shouts brought aid, but it was too late to save Owens.

Owens's heroism was reported worldwide by the Associated Press, and that July he was selected to be a recipient of the Carnegie Hero Fund Commission medal. A swimming complex that once stood on the south end of the park was named in his honor, though it has since been closed. Today, a stone memorial with a bronze marker commemorates Owens's bravery in the park.

There are those who say that Owens's spirit is still watching over the lake. It is clearly posted that no swimming is permitted, but from time to time,

A memorial stands to remind visitors of Owens's bravery. *Provine's collection.*

risk-takers decide to brave the waterfowl and wade in. They return saying they felt a force, even the impressions of small hands, trying to get them out. Not only those who get into the water, but those toeing close to it as well say they can feel Owens pushing them away.

Another spirit can be found in the park in the form of a phantom that walks the eastern side of the lake. A woman wearing a long white dress walks casually, looking aloof as she strolls near the water and even to the bridge. She is almost always seen at a distance and only for a moment before the surprised person blinks and she is gone. One legend goes that she is Robert Lee Owens's mother out looking for him, but Mrs. Owens lived until 2012, long after the rumors of the ghostly woman began. Perhaps, then, she is a visitor to the park from among the generations who have enjoyed it, returning despite her body having passed on.

23
Legends of Imo Cemetery

"Legend tripping" is the ten-dollar term used to describe the activity of going out to explore urban legends. Typically, it's ascribed to teenagers looking to do something on a boring night, but just about anyone can head out to explore the sites of spooky or entertaining stories. Garfield County has a number of legendary destinations to visit but none more famous than the glowing headstone at Imo Cemetery, just a mile east and two miles north of Drummond. The burial grounds lay amid a grove of trees, looking out on the endless wheat fields seen throughout the county. Graves there date as far back as 1897, with people choosing this as their serene resting spot ever since.

The Imo glowing headstone legend goes back to time immemorial. Visitors should arrive on the night of a full moon, stand on the road and look into the cemetery. As they peer over the darkness of the nighttime cemetery, one of the headstones will glow brightly. Visitors should not approach the cemetery, however, since that causes the magic to break and the light to go out. If they back away again, the headstone will glow again.

Many embrace the supernatural explanation that this is the work of a blessed individual whose marker shows a life remembered glowingly, literally. There is some disagreement, however, about which headstone it is, since several of them are said to do it and only at certain angles. This has led other visitors to turn to a more mundane explanation for the glowing. A trip to the cemetery during the day to pay respects will show

Urban legends speak of a glowing headstone, though which one is up to debate. *Provine's collection.*

the obvious answer that some of the headstones are left rough and a few are polished stone. The polished ones catch the light of the moon or the lights of the oil well on the north side of the cemetery. The rough stones don't. Thus, it may be simply a trick of the light that makes one headstone appear to glow among its shadowy neighbors.

Still, the glowing headstone isn't the only legendary light at the cemetery. Several visitors have captured photographs of what has been described as a "demon baby" sneaking behind the headstones. Frequently the photos show a malformed tiny human face, a tint on little wings and a winding tail. Numerous paranormal investigators have visited the cemetery seeking their own answers, wondering if it may be a restless spirit from one of the younger people buried there or something more sinister lurking about the hallowed grounds. Several people have claimed to feel scratches or even bites at their legs. Skeptics, though, suspect that the blurry photos may be another set of reflections from decorations adorning various headstones. They do not have an explanation for the EVPs that capture hissing or dragged-out growls since mortal creatures would've been heard by anyone making the recording.

Still more lights shine in the thick woods surrounding the cemetery. Visitors have frequently seen spooklights among the trees. Also called will-o'-the-wisps or hobby lanterns, these floating orbs of light seem to dance a few feet off the ground without any rational explanation. They, too, react to their viewers, moving backward or up or disappearing as people come closer. No one can find anything that might be reflective like a polished headstone to make them.

Some suggest that the lights are actually the reflection of the eyes of a creature. The light could easily move as it moves its head and even disappear as it looks away. When people go to investigate, the creature moves on, leaving nothing to be found. If it is some creature, it must be huge, as the lights float sometimes six to eight feet up into the air clear of branches where a smaller creature might have climbed. Weathered claw marks on one of the headstones at the back of the cemetery, too, suggest it is huge.

Aside from the lights, investigators at the cemetery have focused on finding explanations for a host of EVPs collected there. Some are whispers, some are animal sounds suggested to be demon babies or dark creatures and some are clear human voices speaking something other than English. One of the legends of the Imo Cemetery is that it was already a burial ground for Native Americans before the land run settlers decided that it was best to continue using the plot that way. The landscape that became Garfield County has been home to Osage, Kiowa, Comanche and many other tribes for centuries, so EVPs seem to support the old story.

As spooky as the legends are, a true story from 1992 brings a different kind of horror. As Halloween approached that fall, the county sheriff's office received a call from the groundskeeper that someone had stolen a body from the cemetery. The *Oklahoman* reported that police arrived to find a hole next to the marker for Martha M. Fair (1824–1910) dug seven feet deep with shovels. Only one human bone remained; the rest were gone. Garfield County undersheriff Ray Pickle stated, "If it's a prank, somebody went to an awful lot of trouble," and they feared it could have been taken for a more sinister reason such as evil rituals. Another mystery arose as to why this one body was taken, since it was old, but not the oldest; nor was there any other perceivable motive. Whatever the terrible reason, the words on Fair's headstone can still offer solace:

Dearest Mother thou hast left us,
And thy loss we deeply feel,
But it is God who has bereaved us,
He will all our sorrows heal.

24
Black Bear's Dark Figures

Surveying from the land run mapped out townships throughout the Outlet, founding more than one hundred towns on a single day in 1893. Unfortunately, towns need real-world resources and transportation connections rather than regular spots on a map to thrive. Towns away from the railroad died out, and some survived by moving, like Coldwater and Hillsdale, which merged when the rail ran straight between them. As populations shifted from rural to urban over the twentieth century, even more of the smaller towns became ghosts, leaving only a few remnants such as grain elevators as markers. More and more disappear each year.

Today in the old Olive Township northeast of Covington there lies a cemetery and the ruins of a church in the blackjack-dotted rolling hills near the eastern edge of the county. Baldwin Cemetery, named for the Baldwins who donated the land from their farm, rests on the north side of the road. It gained the more common name "Black Bear Cemetery" from Black Bear Creek running just a half mile to the south. Across the road there stands the rubble-strewn remains of what had once been New Bethany Baptist Church. Though the roof, doors and flooring are all gone, its blond brick walls are robust, now the canvas for decades of graffiti from simple tags with names to messages or swear words and satanic symbols.

Some of the visitors whisper legends that the old church was shut down after it veered from the straight and narrow path onto an occult road of destruction. More likely, the symbols are a product of the church closing sometime after World War II and its congregation leaving the building

The ruins of a church stand across the road from Black Bear Cemetery. *Provine's collection.*

behind. Interest in alternative religions grew during the latter half of the twentieth century, which unnerved many traditionalists. Conservative backlash in the Satanic Panic of the 1980s stated strange and violent rituals were sweeping the nation, and a curious backlash to the backlash prompted some people to experiment with darker arts, such as performing rites in once-consecrated places. To this day at this old church, animal bones are said to be found in the midst of freshly blackened spots on pillars and concrete where sacrifices took place.

According to legend, the rituals at what is usually nicknamed "Black Bear Church," even though the actual town is in another county, have invited something dark into the area. With its easy access, just five and a half miles east of Highway 74 and a mile and a half south of US-64/412, the church and cemetery are favorites of legend-trippers and paranormal investigators alike. The grounds are private property, and trespassing is sternly punished, so visits should only take place with permission or during daytime respectful observances at the cemetery.

Those who visit the old church come away with unwell feelings and unexplainable evidence of something not right. Numerous paranormal investigators, including researchers and authors Cathy Nance, Logan Corelli and Mike Ricksecker, have been to the site collecting photographs, video and audio recordings and chilling personal experiences. Faces peer out of the windows in pictures, perhaps taken to be reflections except that the glass has long been broken out. Plenty of photographs show orbs, which can often be caused from reflections on dust or fast-moving insects common in the Oklahoma countryside. Other lights cannot so easily be explained, including one that seemed to hang over the roofless church walls, visible from several angles before it disappeared.

The church's basement is particularly terrifying. Even beyond the regular spookiness of shadowy, cold, underground spaces, this one seems to give a sensation of horror. One EVP captured by an investigation team even whispered plainly, "You shouldn't be here." Other EVPs include women's voices, maniacal laughter and an assortment of inhuman growls, many of which cannot be associated with any known animal. Those who have gone into the basement have felt being touched, scratched and even struck by unseen hands. One investigator was even pushed hard enough to fall several feet from where he was standing.

As if disembodied sounds and ghostly touches weren't enough, the church is most famous for the dark figures that lurk. Some are humanoid shadows, walking as if impressions from churchgoers past before fading from view. The most terrifying figure is a "crawler," a term used by investigators for a human-sized visible entity that scampers low on long limbs. The crawler at the church ruin has been seen to scuttle along the ground out into the brush or behind corners. Some have seen it run up the walls and then out into the open air where the roof had once been, scurrying as if it still felt the tiles under its claws.

The Black Bear Cemetery offers friendlier spirits. The well-kept grounds serve as peaceful final resting places for folks whose graves bear some dates going back over one hundred years and some very recently. One marker in the northwest corner reads simply, "Unknown Cowboy," lending ground for someone that no one could name but felt the neighborly need to bury. Here EVPs and psychic sessions have greeted several spirits, including those who warn about not messing with the things across the road. Other conversations are much more genial. In his *Ghosts and Legends of Oklahoma* web series, Ricksecker recalled the time he was noting that John L. Allen had two markers, one with his wife and one provided by the U.S. Navy. While Ricksecker commented on the two, an EVP pointed out, "Correct."

The energetic spirits of the church and cemetery do not always seem to stay put, either. Footsteps echo on the gravel road even when it is empty

Glowing eyes are said to peer from the thicket behind Black Bear Cemetery. *Provine's collection.*

for miles in either direction. One group said it saw a squat dark figure only a few feet tall and far wider at the back of the cemetery. When they went to investigate, it took off and then leaped ten feet into the trees, where it watched them with glowing red eyes. They continued looking for it, but flashlights showed nothing physical for the eyes to be attached to.

Beyond straying on their own, the spirits can follow those who visit. Visitors who have gotten terrible feelings, even crying and vomiting from the stress, said that the invading darkness continued even elsewhere until they underwent cleansing with sage and other sacraments. Others say they heard footsteps following behind them, crunches in the gravel when everyone living had stopped. One investigation team felt someone unseen climb into the car with them. They shouted at it, telling it they refused permission for it to go with them and sprinkled oil. The car then shifted as if something got out through the open door though there was nothing to be seen.

25
Beasts of Garfield County

On the north side of the county, there was one story the older folks loved to tell grandkids about the times when they were their age—that of the Hillsdale Monster. There were numerous descriptions of the beast: six feet tall, huge legs, a thick tail, flashing eyes set in a pointed, tiny head. Anyone who saw it might recognize it as a kangaroo, something rarely found on the Great Plains. It was said to have escaped from a circus train passing through in the 1930s, and it hid out in the creek bottoms and draws. Several hunters went after it, but the creature proved elusive. Those who did see it, either purposefully or on accident, were so surprised that they couldn't get a bead on it before it bounded away. The legend goes that the monster was never caught. It either wandered off, or the winters got it, or it may still be hiding out, waiting for an unsuspecting kid to wander too close to the shadows and then…GULP!

There was another creature story, too, that was repeated with much less mirth because it was no laughing matter: the Black Beast of Kremlin.

In early 1952, farmers began discovering calves and sheep massacred in the fields between Kremlin and Pond Creek. Aside from the financial loss and the sickening brutality, it was the fact that it kept happening that most worried farmers. For generations, hunters had thinned out predators like coyotes to the point that seeing one was a novelty. This creature responsible for the killings was far larger than a coyote, something big and hungry that had moved into the area.

Judging from the marks on the cattle remains, police determined the animal was a large cat. Large cats have long been part of the Great Plains, whether people prefer the term "mountain lion" or "cougar" or "panther" for the blanket term for large cats. In the early days, people could regularly hear the haunting scream of a cougar in the night. It was common enough that Marquis James noted "panther" being on his list of vocabulary words to correct his pronunciation from the more colloquial "painther" that he'd picked up from less refined types while living outside of town. Following settlement, large cats became fairly rare in Oklahoma. In fact, for many years, official reports have maintained that there were no mountain lions in the state at all. Those who claimed to have seen a mountain lion were assured it was likely a bobcat or even a large barn cat. Trail cameras catching cats on film could be difficult to confirm the size, so huge news came in 2021 when one posed for the camera alongside a porcupine near Canton, showing big cats do prowl Oklahoma.

In 1952, after years of quiet, people began hearing the beast's cry in the night. Eyewitnesses said that they had seen the enormous cat, but only just a glimpse, since its especially dark coat made it nearly invisible at night. For the most part, the only thing that people could see was its flashing yellow eyes before even those disappeared into the night. One driver who saw the full beast on the blacktop west of Kremlin with his headlights panicked and ended up deep in the ditch. Herds were brought in from the pasture at night, and no one left the house after dark. Hunters from three states came to track the beast.

Mountain lions stalk northern Oklahoma, as trail cam footage from 2021 shows. *Courtesy of Jacquie Holt.*

Of course, not everyone took the threat so seriously. Howard Kirkpatrick recounted his memories of taking advantage of the public fear of the beast in the 2016 oral history project by Kremlin-Hillsdale High School in which students interviewed elders, *Story Matters*, edited by Peggy Harris. Kirkpatrick told how he and his buddies made a panther from cardboard and black paint with pieces of mirrors for its shining eyes. After testing their design out one night, they decided they couldn't be convinced and tossed it under the bridge one mile east of Kremlin just to be rid of it.

Later that night, they "were listening to a basketball game on the radio when the reporter broke into the broadcast and announced that the panther had been seen one mile east of Kremlin." The boys piled into Kirkpatrick's '36 Chevrolet to retrieve their model cat before it caused any more trouble. While driving back into town with it over the front fender, they passed the highway patrol cruising with spotlights scanning for the creature. If not for a deft turn, they might've been caught.

The story made the newspapers, and the boys came clean. Even though their episode of the panther epic was a prank, it brought light to even more tragedy. Numerous farmers recounted their losses, and locals were thankful no humans had been victims. One of the hunters noted that he had spotted one of the boys' barefoot prints under the bridge where he had run to grab the cardboard critter. It was near large cat prints that led up the creek a half mile before the trail went cold. The news reports related that eyewitnesses described the creature as having a "big bushy tail." The boys' painted cardboard cat didn't have a tail. Something else was out prowling that night, and even a few minutes' difference might have crossed their paths.

An estimated two thousand to five thousand hunters and seven surveillance planes combed the county for the black beast, but it slipped by them all. Eventually, the stories of the black beast dried up. A new drought was settling in, one that would plague farmers all through the '50s. Likely the creature had grown too large for its habitat and was moving on now that farmers were keeping a protective eye on their herds. Folks were glad to have it gone.

Researcher Jim Whitehead tells of another, much larger creature that has been sighted stalking the county: bigfoot. These hairy humanoid beasts have been seen all over, drinking from cattle ponds near Garber to crossing dirt roads south of Lahoma to rifling through trash cans on the outskirts of Enid. It's no new thing, either: in 1912, a road crew clearing brush was chased off by an enormous stinking ape-man that later attacked a horse and buggy, injuring the horse such that it died. So many have been seen between Waukomis and Covington that neighbors have dubbed it the "Hackberry

Creek Monster" and discuss differences in size, color and smell, suggesting there may be more than one monster venturing up the creek.

Many of the sightings overlap the ghost legends of Garfield County, with bigfoot making appearances in the dense trees behind Imo Cemetery or two child-sized bigfoots scampering away in the brush near Black Bear Cemetery. Even reports of the Black Beast of Kremlin suggested that it wasn't catlike but a long-legged ape that walked on two feet, though its eyes still flashed in the darkness.

Whether ghost or cryptid, there are always more stories of Garfield County to take in.

BIBLIOGRAPHY

Books

Bates, Finis L. *The Escape and Suicide of John Wilkes Booth*. Naperville, IL: Nichols, 1907.

Corelli, Logan. *The Haunted Heart of America*. Woodbury, MN: Llewellyn Publications, 2018.

Farris, David A. *More Mysterious Oklahoma*. Edmond, OK: Little Bruce, 2001.

James, Marquis. *The Cherokee Strip*. Norman: University of Oklahoma Press, 1945.

Johnson, Byron Berkeley. *Abraham Lincoln and Boston Corbett: With Personal Recollections of Each; John Wilkes Booth and Jefferson Davis, A True Story of Their Capture*. Waltham, MA: B.B. Johnson, 1914.

Mahoney, Ella V. *Sketches of Tudor Hall and the Booth Family*. Bel Air, MD: Tudor Hall, 1925.

McIntyre, Glen V. *Enid: 1893–1945*. Charleston, SC: Arcadia Publishing, 2012.

Morris, John Wesley. *Ghost Towns of Oklahoma*. Norman: University of Oklahoma Press, 1978.

Rockwell, Stella, ed. *Garfield County, Oklahoma, 1907–1982*, Vol. 1. Topeka, KS: Garfield Historical Society, Josten's Publishing Company, 1982.

———. *Garfield County, Oklahoma, 1893–1982*, Vol. 2. Topeka, KS: Garfield Historical Society, Josten's Publishing Company, 1982.

Savage, William W., Jr. *The Cherokee Strip Live Stock Association*. Norman: University of Oklahoma Press, 1990.

Articles

Barron, Robert. "Local Masonic Lodge Opened Year After Cherokee Strip Run." *Enid News & Eagle*, December 13, 2009.
Castleman, Jack. "Courthouse Burning Closed Stormy Chapter in History." *Enid Morning News*, February 21, 1971.
Cimarron Valley Clipper. May 19, 1904.
Culver, Galen. "Garfield County Jail Art." KFOR. January 14, 2021.
Cummings, Joe. "A Daring Spirit." *Enid News & Eagle*, August 12, 2018.
———. "'No Greater Manhunt'—Almost Never-Ending Manhunt Continues for Zip Wyatt." *Enid News & Eagle*, August 19, 2018.
———. "'Oklahoma Giant' and 'Little Nick:' The True Stories of Lewis Wilkins and Nicu de Barcsy." *Enid News & Eagle*, November 8, 2020.
Cunningham, Robert. "The Town Without Men." *Oklahoman*, February 19, 1961.
Enid Buzz. "Hauntings & Lore." N.d.
Enid Echo. "Deaths." January 14, 1903.
———. "Slayer of the Beloved President." January 21, 1903.
Enid Morning News. "Big Cat, Cougar Perhaps, Is Keeping Farmers Wide Awake." February 2, 1952.
Enid Weekly Wave. "The Booth Matter." June 11, 1903.
———. "Booth Matter Again." June 4, 1903.
———. "Booth vs. George." January 22, 1903.
———. "The City Council." January 6, 1894.
———. "Decoration Day." June 2, 1898.
———. "A Double Affliction." August 11, 1894.
———. "Enid His Home." June 28, 1900.
———. "The Ghost Story." September 13, 1906.
———. "A Haunted Cell." December 15, 1894.
———. "Is It Booth?" January 22, 1903.
———. "J. Wilkes Booth." January 22, 1903.
———. "Leaden-heeled Law." January 15, 1903.
———. "Mayor's Message." April 11, 1895.
———. "Took a Grave Yard Fence." December 9, 1897.
Farris, David. "Law Enforcement Badly Wanted Zip Wyatt." *Edmond Life & Leisure*, April 23, 2015.
Garber Sentinel. "The Fake Murder." December 5, 1918.
———. "A Ghost Story." February 11, 1915.
———. "Mystery Unsolved." January 22, 1903.

Garfield County Democrat. "George Is Not Booth." June 11, 1903.

———. "George Told His Story Here." February 5, 1903.

Jerman, Emily. "Single Frontier Women Took Park in Oklahoma 1893 Land Run." *Oklahoma Gazette*, June 3, 2009.

Kirkpatrick, Howard, and Cooper Coffey. "Cat Caper." *Story Matters*. Ed. Peggy Harris. 2016.

McKenzie, Birdie. "Society." *Enid Daily Eagle*, November 2, 1908.

McNutt, Michael. "Body Stolen from Grave at Enid Area Cemetery." *Oklahoman*, October 28, 1992.

News9. "Oklahomans Capture Video of Mountain Lions on Trail Cams." October 25, 2021.

New York Times. "Annetta Daisy's Amazons." April 16, 1892.

Nichols, Max. "State Oil and Gas History on Display in Oklahoma." *The Oklahoman*, January 29, 2012.

North Enid Tribune. "Round Pond." February 22, 1894.

Pond Creek Tribune. "Bold Train Robbers." April 12, 1894.

"Ruth Monro Augur's Murals." Enid Arts Council, August 2014.

San Antonio Light. "Texas, Unable to Score, Bows to Haymakers, Phillips University Blanks Longhorns on Muddy Field 10 to 0." October 12, 1919.

Whitehead, Jim. "Enid." Unpublished.

Government Documents

Berry, Robert. "Broadway Tower." National Register of Historic Places. July 10, 1984.

Warde, Mary Jane. "Enid Cemetery and Calvary Catholic Cemetery." National Register of Historic Places. January 15, 1994.

Television

Ghost Lab. "John Wilkes Booth." Season 1, episode 6. November 10, 2009.

Web

Boucher, Kurtis W., and Richard A. Marston. "Great Salt Plains." *Encyclopedia of Oklahoma History of Culture*. https://www.okhistory.org.

Brown, Gary L. "Enid." *Encyclopedia of Oklahoma History and Culture*. https://www.okhistory.org.

Donnab's Weblog. "Enid's Legend of Dollie Douthitt." https://dmbr622.wordpress.com.

Everett, Dianna. "Hillsdale." *Encyclopedia of Oklahoma History and Culture*. https://www.okhistory.org.

———. "Waukomis." *Encyclopedia of Oklahoma History and Culture*. https://www.okhistory.org.

Haunted Road Media. *Ghosts and Legends of Oklahoma*. "Episode 4: Black Bear Church and Cemetery." December 18, 2014. https://www.youtube.com.

Liminal Space. inaliminalspace.org.

Longfellow Middle School. "History of Longfellow." https://lms.enidpublicschools.org.

McIntyre, Glen V. "Phillips University." *Encyclopedia of Oklahoma History and Culture*. https://www.okhistory.org.

OKPRI. "BlackBear Church." https://www.okpri.com.

Post-Mortem Investigators. "IMO Cemetery - Drummond Oklahoma." January 28, 2020. https://post-morteminvestigators.com.

Pratt, Kay. "Off the Beaten Path—Skeleton Creek Ranch, Enid." https://www.kaypratt.com.

SpikeDiegel. "May 11, 2014 Black Bear Church." YouTube. May 13, 2014. https://www.youtube.com.

Tales Unveiled. "The Tombstone Tales of Enid." Produced by The Show Starts Now Studios. November 15, 2019. https://www.talesunveiled.com.

Turner, Alvin O. "Cherokee Outlet Opening." *Encyclopedia of Oklahoma History and Culture*. https://www.okhistory.org.

Weaver, Bobby D. "North Enid." *Encyclopedia of Oklahoma History and Culture*. https://www.okhistory.org.

About the Authors

Tammy Wilson, Enid resident, has had a love for haunted history for as long as she can remember. She has investigated many haunted locations around the country and co-wrote *Ghostlahoma—100 Years of Oklahoma's Haunted History* with Tonya Hacker. She researches Oklahoma ghost towns and obscure and strange places to travel within the state.

Tammy owns a business located in a one-hundred-year-old building in historic downtown Enid, as well as the Enid Event Company. She conducts the Eerie Enid Ghost Tours and plans festivals and events throughout the year. Her activism in the community led to an eight-year stint on the City Commission where she was also a charter member of the Public Art Commission of Enid. She has served on the Gaslight Theatre Board of Directors and is an active member of the theater.

Tammy is married and has four adult children and one spoiled English Mastiff. She enjoys road trips and adventures.

Jeff Provine grew up on his family's Land Run farm just north of Hillsdale and today serves as a professor of English at Oklahoma City Community College. While spending a year abroad in England, Jeff soaked up as many local tours as he could and became inspired to seek

out Oklahoma's own legends. The project has grown into guided ghost tours in Norman and Oklahoma City and several collections of folklore, including *Campus Ghosts of Norman*, *Haunted Norman*, *Haunted Guthrie*, *Haunted Oklahoma City*, *Haunted Shawnee* and *Haunted Oklahoma*. He has appeared on the Travel Channel's *Famously Afraid* and serves as cohost with Dennis Spielman for Tales Unveiled, a docu-narrative exploring the legends of Oklahoma.

In addition to nonfiction work, Jeff produces comics, including the *Okie Comics* magazine featuring Oklahoma artists telling Oklahoma stories, and speculative fiction. Jeff may be found online at www.jeffprovine.com and facebook.com/authorjeffprovine as well as twitter.com/jeffprovine, where he posts #vss very short stories.